A MAN AND HIS MOTHER

A MAN AND HIS MOTHER

An Adopted Son's Search

Tim Green

ReganBooks

An Imprint of HarperCollinsPublishers

HarperCollins books may be purchased for educational, business, or sales promotional use. For information please write: Special Markets Department, HarperCollins Publishers, Inc., 10 East 53rd Street, New York, NY 10022.

FIRST EDITION

Designed by Elina D. Nudelman

Library of Congress Cataloging-in-Publication Data
Green, Tim, 1963–
    A man and his mother : an adopted son's search / Tim Green.
      p.   cm.
    ISBN 0-06-039217-7
    1. Adopted children—United States—Biography. 2. Mothers and sons—United States. I. Title.
    HV874.82.G74A3   1997
    362.73'4'092—dc21   97-28465
[B]

97 98 99 00 01 ❖/RRD 10 9 8 7 6 5 4 3 2 1

This is a true story. However, in order to protect the privacy of certain individuals, some names and identifying details have been changed.

A MAN AND HIS MOTHER

One

When my college girlfriend broke up with me, the first thing I did was go tell her mother. My relationship with Audry was probably as important to me as the one I had with her daughter. In fact, the day I met Beth was also the same day I met Audry. Beth I found on the beach, and by the end of the day I had finagled my way into a cold drink beside the pool of her family's oceanfront home. It was late in the afternoon when Audry appeared with her husband, Neil, home from a barbecue in Avalon. Audry wore a pair of tan summer slacks and a silk short-sleeved top. Her bearing was regal, but her smile, like her pale green eyes, was warm and ingenuous. Except for the nearly inconspicuous crow's-feet, she looked nothing like the middle-aged mother she was. I knew instantly where Beth had gotten her looks.

I got off the lounge chair and politely shook both parents' hands, a reflection of the manners my own parents demanded and a good way to earn brownie points from the get-go. We talked, Beth's parents and I. I told them where I was from, how I happened to be visiting the Jersey Shore, and what my general prospects in life appeared to be at that time. I was a scholarship athlete attending Syracuse University. In other words, big-time football. But I liked school too, always an important detail to relate to the parents of a potential girlfriend. Three years later, Audry would remind me that I also disclosed the fact I was an adopted child. I have no recollection of that, but it would become obvious, because of the impact it had on her, that I did indeed tell them.

Not only did I impress the parents that day, I impressed Beth as well. It was destiny that she was to attend Cornell that coming fall. Although, the truth be known, Cornell was not an uncommon destination for well-heeled girls from New Jersey. While my relationship with Beth was often tumultuous, her family was a different story. They embraced me, especially Audry. By the following year, I made it my business to secure a summer job in Manhattan so I could actually live with Beth and her family in Englewood during June and July.

On weekends, we would retreat, like one big family, to their palatial summer home on the Jersey Shore. Her sister was younger and pleasant, although too like Beth in her independence to dote over me. But she liked me enough to show it. Neil, the father, was an operator. He owned a Mercedes dealership as well as a couple of restaurants around Englewood. If there was a hot car, he had to have it, and it didn't have to be a Mercedes. Whenever the bill came after dinner? He carried a fat roll of hundred-dollar bills in his pocket that he'd peel off like the leaves of a cabbage. But while Beth's father and younger sister clearly approved of my presence, it was Audry, more than even Beth herself, who seemed delighted.

During the summer weeks, I worked a soft PR job at the firm of a prominent SU alum who was more concerned with my progress in the weight room than in public relations. After the job—and three hours of hard training at the gym—I'd end up back at Beth's. It was Audry, not Beth, who would break into the refrigerator and whip together a meal. I'm talking about real food: pasta with homemade sauce; veal cutlets sautéed in white wine; or a fat steak cooked on the grill, served with french fried potatoes. It never seemed to matter to Audry that she'd spent her day working at one of Neil's restaurants. She was that kind of woman. Despite their money, Audry did all the cooking and all the cleaning. Every day she did the work of at least two, if not three, normal women. Looking back now, I suppose this was one of the ways in which she punished herself. Then, I had no idea that she felt she should be punished. In my mind, her exacting work ethic and blind devotion to the rest of us made her the perfect wife. I fully expected Beth to mature into that same role.

Of course, I tried to stay on my best behavior those summers, but when I inevitably slipped into my worst, drinking too much beer on a Friday night or wrecking a jet ski out of carelessness, it was Audry again, not Beth, who was my champion. She seemed to revel in my recklessness and was always quick to remind Beth that, in general, I was a model young man. Over the three years that I knew them, it became clear to everyone in Beth's family that Audry gave me preferential treatment. If Beth and I had a dispute, Audry would come down on my side of the argument. If there was only one Dove bar left in the freezer, she wanted to make sure I didn't want it first. She was my mentor as well. While my own parents never left me short on manners, I had no sense of style. It was Audry who went out of her way to buy me nice clothes and instruct me how best to get by in the social setting of the well-to-do.

It wasn't unusual on a Saturday night for the two of us to stay up later than everyone else, talking at the kitchen table about books or politics or psychology or just the people we'd been with that day at their summer house. Under an old brass hanging lamp, we'd sit, separated from the night by only a sliding screen door. The hypnotic sounds of the surf carried in to us on the ocean breeze. If the wind was stiff, the heavy old fixture would gently sway, leaving the shadows to dance a slow tango across the floor. An easy current ran between the two of us in those moments, as if we were coconspirators in some secret but noble cause. I understood her and she understood me. When we talked, we looked into each other's eyes with the comfort of two old friends, unafraid to expose our thoughts and ideas.

It was there, alone in her kitchen, that I read aloud my first piece of fiction, a short story I'd cobbled together during the week at my PR job in the city.

"I'm going to be a writer," I explained, finishing off the bottle of beer I'd begun for courage. Nothing in her voice or expression that night told me that I couldn't.

When it became late, my eyes would sag and my words would wander aimlessly. Audry would get up from the table, kiss me on top of my head, and tell me to go to sleep.

"Tomorrow's another day," she'd say. Then she'd make off to bed with an impish smile and a spring in her step that suggested she had no need of sleep herself, that rest was only for the young.

During those summer months of my college days, I became a real part of Beth's family, and I grew to love her mother. All that time, I attributed Audry's unusual kindness to the fact that I was a guest. The real reason was never even a suspect, until the day I went to say good-bye.

Beth and I looked like a good couple, and in truth, we had fun together. But that was only when we weren't bickering. For all my macho football-star veneer, I was frantically insecure, especially when it came to Beth. Naturally, I did my best to hold her tight. I liked to know where she was every minute of every day. I wanted to be with her all the time, as much as anything so that I could keep an eye on her. I was insanely jealous and a poor fit for a girl whose theme song was Lynyrd Skynyrd's "Free Bird."

At the end of the summer before I was to enter my senior year, Beth finally had had enough. On the warm sunny day I was to return to Syracuse to begin football camp, she told me she wanted to start seeing other people at school. I tried begging. I tried bullying. It was the steely look in her eyes that finally convinced me it was no use. We were finished.

I felt it was only right that I break the news to Audry in person. After all, I wouldn't be seeing her again. As much as I may have deluded myself about my relationship with Beth, I wasn't too far gone to know that along with the breakup, Audry and I would be permanently disunited. My summer was over. I was heading back to school. My car was packed. Before I got onto the highway, I stopped by the restaurant to say good-bye.

Audry came out from the kitchen for some reason other than to see me. When she did see me, her smile melted away.

"What's wrong, Tim?"

"I need to talk to you," I said quietly.

A couple of waitresses were setting some tables, and they stopped to stare. Audry gave them a curt look, letting them know it was time to get back to work, then led me out through a glass door and into the deserted courtyard that was the centerpiece of the restaurant. The thin ornamental trees and decorative white crushed stones did little to relieve the heat from the late afternoon sun. Our bodies and clothes absorbed the heat as if it were a liquid. I sat down on a concrete bench and rested my arms across the tops of my thighs. I stared into the crushed stone.

"What's wrong?" she asked.

"Well," I replied, choking back a myriad of emotions with a heavy sigh, "I think I won't be seeing you that much anymore."

My stomach was knotted in sadness. I couldn't help it. I'd known this woman for three years. I'd spent every summer with her and her family. In that time, she had treated me like a son.

"Beth and I are breaking up. I wanted to tell you in person. I wanted you to know how much I appreciate everything you've done for me. I'm going to miss you. . . . "

I dared to look up at her then. Silent contagious tears were streaming down her face. It seemed there was something else happening inside her, as if it were more than saying good-bye to her daughter's boyfriend, even one she really liked. There was.

She stepped close, and I stood up so she could hug me to her. I was suddenly aware of how small a woman she was—or how large I was. She made me think of a delicate Lalique figure. It was as if prior to that moment I had only observed her from a distance, with a poor perception of depth. Suddenly, she pulled away from me as if to compose herself, looking up into the hot sky with her weeping eyes half shut and fluttering.

"I have to tell you something," she said, looking back to me and holding my hands in her own. "No one knows this, not even my own children."

Her eyes bore into mine. Her look and her words slowed the moment, as if part of a dream.

"Did you ever wonder why I've treated you the way I have?" she whispered.

I shrugged. I was acutely aware of the rings on her fingers and the soft strength in her hands.

"You've been like a mother to me," I sputtered, embarrassed now, but curious.

"Yes," she said distantly, "like a mother . . . "

I waited so long for her to speak that I began to think she might not. Finally, she sighed heavily and said, "The first day I met you, you told me you were adopted. I don't remember how it came up, but it did. I couldn't believe it at first. It seemed so strange to me that there you were in my life. . . . "

The dreamy quality of her voice ended abruptly.

"When I was in college," she told me, "I got pregnant, and I had a baby boy that I gave up for adoption."

I looked at her incredulously, a million things racing through my mind.

"No," she said. "You're not my son. He's older than you are. I don't know where he is. I probably never will know. . . . "

She looked off and I waited again.

"He was Neil's son too," she said in an indirect way, as if she were hypnotized or speaking to some unseen third party. "The girls' brother. They don't know. No one knows.

"When I got pregnant, I wasn't married. It was different back then. Something you didn't do. After that, after I had the baby and gave him up, the only man I felt I could marry was Neil. We talked about trying to get him back, but it was too late. It was impossible.

"Then we started our own family. We had the girls. I tried to forget about him. And I mostly did. Then I met you, and there was something about you . . . you seemed so . . . I don't know, lost? So . . . alone."

Now she looked at me directly again and said, "I loved you like him. I don't know if he's all right. I don't know if he's happy. I hope he is . . . I wish I knew. . . . "

I grabbed hold of her and held her tight. She shook against my frame. There was nothing I could say. I loved her, too. For the way she had treated me, I knew I always would. She was one of the finest women I've ever met. And it was in that moment that an idea pierced my mind like the shaft of a lightning bolt.

Somewhere, only God knew where, but somewhere, there was a woman who was my mother. Maybe she was a woman like this one. Maybe she was as warm and kind and generous as this woman. Maybe she too ached deep down for a scrap of news, just a bit of information that would let her know that what she'd done had been the right thing, that the son she gave away was happy.

Until that moment, I had never consciously considered the mother who gave me away. Thinking beyond the parents who raised me was something I'd never allowed myself to do. So why now was I willing, after twenty-one years, to shake the foundation of my life? Was it only because I was thinking about it from a mother's point of view for the first time, or was there something more? To find the answer, I would have to go back to the beginning.

Two

On the first night of practice, I had the excitement that only children seem able to possess. I squirmed in the front seat of my father's forest-green station wagon as we pulled into the dusty parking lot. Adjacent to us was a long grassy field lit in the golden-orange glow of a summer evening. On either end of the field were goalposts. They were not painted luminescent yellow like the ones I'd seen on TV; they were white and pocked with brown rust, soccer goals with two unwieldy antennae.

I was eight and didn't care. In my lap rested the bright white shell of a real football helmet. Its pungent plastic odor was new to me. It spoke of important things to come. Of course, I had played football in the neighbors' yards dozens of times. But this was the beginning of something altogether different. This was real, organized football. Little League. I would have coaches. Granted, they were nothing more than enthusiastic fathers, but we would call them "coach." They would carry shiny whistles around their necks that screeched authoritatively. They would make us run and roll and hop and even crawl.

"Okay," my father said, "good luck."

"Okay."

I nodded and let myself out of the car without looking back. I didn't expect him to stay and watch. It wasn't that he didn't care, and it wasn't that he was too ashamed of me (despite his doubts about my being even a Little League football player). My father was a pragmatic man, and it made no sense to watch a practice, especially when it was conveniently located a half mile from the library. He could drop me off, get his books for the week, and easily make it back in time to watch us run a final lap around the field.

I walked tentatively into the loose circle of waiting boys, some of whom had taken to playing recklessly, the way boys will when they know each other well. Although I was the same size as the rest of them, I didn't know a soul. I didn't recognize a face or a name. Suddenly, the whole thing didn't seem like it was going to be any fun at all—and it wasn't. I did my best to keep up with the others, but every one of them could catch and run and hit and hustle better than I could.

This confused me, because in the neighborhood I was indomitable. If there was an odd number of boys playing a game in the Wongs' front yard, I would always count for two. That night, I didn't even count for one. I struggled and slipped. I wore sneakers instead of cleated shoes like everyone else, and the thick summer grass was slick like wet autumn leaves on a road.

I would play for the entire season like that, slipping and sliding, especially when it was wet. Mud was my nemesis. My parents weren't going to buy me an expensive pair of football cleats if I wasn't going to stick with it. I didn't blame them for that any more than I blamed my father for not staying to watch. I still don't. I knew my parents weren't frugal—I'll never forget my mother coming home one day with brand-new skateboards, the latest neighborhood fad, for me and my brother—but they were careful with money, and I had never given them any reason whatsoever to believe that I had the temperament to be a football player. To spend $30 on a pair of cleats I would only wear six times in my life (the number of games in our season) was certainly not pragmatic.

My father was a big enough fan of the game to know that size wasn't everything. I was the kind of kid who fell down the stairs from time to time, tripped on the rug, and couldn't throw a snowball to save myself. During my early childhood, I slept in orthopedic braces, clanking myself to sleep almost every night, railing against the leather and metal that was supposed to correct the abnormal alignment of my lower legs. My parents never even knew for sure if I would be able to walk normally, let alone run on a football field.

But more important than all that, I was timid. I was a big kid, yes, but my cowardice seemed to outsize even my boatlike feet. I was afraid of the dark, afraid to go down into the basement or even to my bedroom upstairs if no one else was there. And I was deathly afraid to fight, a quality that seems essential to being a good football player. My mother still tells the story to this day of how as a child I appeared at the front door one day in tears, as usual.

"What's wrong, Tim?" she asked, irritated.

"He . . . he . . ." I sobbed, "he took my bike. . . . "

"Who, Tim?"

"Alex, Alex took my b-bike," I wailed.

My mother, a German-American woman with the Teutonic toughness of a good, hardy country girl, furrowed her brow and marched off down the street with me in tow.

Now, I was more scared of my mother than I was of Alex—or of anyone else for that matter. Not as a rule, but when she got that look, I was scared. While my father seemed to drift at times through life, my mother chugged about with a freshly stoked boiler. She made me take that bike back, just take it. It was amazing how it worked: You just stood up for yourself and people backed right down. Amazing. Of course, I never really learned to do it well until much later in life, at a time when I towered over my mother. (Admittedly, it was my wife, a diminutive woman of 5'4", who really taught me to stand up for myself. And even now, the ease with which she can back down a bully mystifies me. Whether it's a belligerent store clerk or an ill-tempered doctor twice her size, my wife just mows them down.)

But that wasn't my nature. So why should my parents have entertained the notion that I would be a football player, that I would last through a season, a game, or even a practice for that matter? I would, though. I did. Yes, I was quick to cry and slow to anger, but because football and books were the two things that were revered in our household, I was determined to be a football player and a writer. That was my childhood dream. So even though I slipped and fell and cried on the football field—and even though my penmanship was so poor my teachers wondered if I could even write my name, let alone a book—there was something inside me that pushed me to get up and go on with renewed determination after each setback.

My dream of being a football player was born from an image I acquired in our family room one Sunday afternoon. My father, normally a quiet, equable man, was maniacally absorbed in the image that filled the TV screen. I was never afraid of my father, but I knew enough to avoid asking inane questions when a game was on. That was akin to stepping on the paw of a normally peaceable old dog: You were sure to get snapped at. It didn't take long for me to realize the power of football.

But it was on that day that I began to understand why my quiet father was so captivated. On the TV, in a gleaming white-and-green uniform, was a blond-haired Philadelphia Eagles linebacker. His face fended off the cold with a thick beard. Dark patches of eye-black smeared in haphazard blotches like two bad shiners made him look forlorn and determined. Steam rose from his head and neck like the smoke from a brush fire. Blood seeped from his mouth and dribbled down his chin like an idiot's spittle; it filled the spaces between his teeth like a movie monster. Incredulously, he smiled, and I began to understand the allure of the game.

My father wasn't the macho type. He didn't drink or brag or treat my mother with anything but respect. Still, he was mesmerized by that television image. In fact, he sat there every Sunday, rain or shine, and it wasn't hard for me to imagine how strong his love and admiration would be for me if one day I was that player. If I could look like a warrior, treat the blood that ran from my body with the same disdain, and smile in the face of pain, not only would my father admire me, I imagined everyone would.

My need to write sprung from the same source. More than football, my parents were enraptured by books. Every Monday they would drive to the public library after dinner and come back with bags full of books. Instead of television in the evenings, the two of them would sit in the family room in their respective chairs reading. Again, it was like football: If you didn't have something important to say, you didn't pester my parents when they were reading. It was early in my life when I began to imagine them one day sitting, enthralled by *my* words, *my* books. I would captivate them completely if I could only write.

I wanted to be a football player as much as I wanted to write books, as much as I wanted to be famous, as much as I wanted not only my parents but the whole world to admire, love, and adore me. In the lonely moments of boyhood, I would stew over these things more than I would worry about getting a new bicycle or the right brand of tennis shoes. Something made me want these things in a way that was permanent. They weren't ephemeral thoughts, nothing like wistfully thinking that you'd love to win the lottery. My need for acceptance and admiration sprung from a deeper source. So naturally, that first night of football practice, when those things seemed far-flung, was quite painful.

"Hey kid."

I looked up at the coach through the plastic face mask of my ill-fitting helmet. He wore a baggy pair of beige work pants and a white sweat-laced T-shirt that stretched across the limits of his beer belly. The only thing missing was an open can of Pabst Blue Ribbon. His hair was thinning on top, and he called his son "Butch." Butch, of course, was the quarterback, and this man was our head coach. I was "kid."

"How old are you, kid?" he said gruffly. He'd been watching me wilt next to the efforts of the others throughout that first practice.

"Eight," I whispered.

His eyes sparkled at that news, and he began to speak in a patronizing tone, like a man playing Santa to a retarded kid.

"Oh, okay, you're okay, then," he said kindly. He knew that players were assigned to one of three divisions in the league according to their body weight. It's just that no one had anticipated an eight-year-old who weighed over a hundred pounds. "You're a little young is all. You've never played football, have you?"

"No," I said. I knew he wouldn't count the Wongs' front lawn.

"No, this is your first year?"

I nodded. That's what I'd said.

"We need to get you down on the lower field next time. That's where the eight-year-olds are. What's your name, kid?"

"Tim. Tim Green," I replied, ashamed for some unknown reason and, of course, a little afraid to be talking with this big burly man who called his son "Butch." What kind of man would do that, after all? Not my father. My father wore a neatly trimmed beard and mustache that were already turning gray. He wore glasses and smoked a gnarled root of a pipe. His own father had been the principal in the small town where he grew up. The boys called my father "Prof," short for professor. He looked like a professor.

"Who are your parents?"

"Richard Green and Judy Green," I said dutifully.

"I think I know who they are," he said, figuring.

I swallowed hard and looked down. I knew what was coming. If he knew them, then he either knew about me or he soon would. I was already old enough to know that I didn't bear the slightest resemblance to a single leaf in my family tree. He would now ask the same question that everyone else always asked. Everyone. Not always out of cruelty, not always out of ignorance, although that certainly happened. But most times people asked because they just couldn't help themselves. As a race, we are curious beings, and a boy who doesn't quite fit the picture is a special curiosity.

"How come you're so big?"

His words hung about me like a fog, refusing to dissipate.

"You're a big kid," he explained, as if I was daft as well as big. He already knew I was clumsy. "Your parents aren't big at all. . . . "

If I had any gusto, the kind of gusto I already knew from one short practice that Butch had, I wouldn't have felt compelled to answer that question. An unanswered question is often a polite way of saying "mind your own business." But, of course, I could no sooner have done that than I could take back my own bicycle. Instead, I confessed.

"I was adopted," I said to him in a whisper.

He looked at me sympathetically. Obviously, a tragedy lay in some nearby shallow grave. This man was polite enough not to ask if I'd ever taken the trouble to dig it up. Many people weren't so kind.

Many people—teachers, other coaches, friends, parents of friends, even strangers—would insist on digging for me, unable to resist the possibility of a glance at some horrible thing.

"When were you *adopted*?"

"How long have you *known*?"

"Who are your *real* parents?"

"Do you want to find *them*?"

The questions rang out in my mind as I waited for them to rain down on me like a sudden shower.

I don't ever remember not knowing that I was adopted, but I was never more aware than on the first day of school. I was five. I stood with the rest of the kindergarten children at the end of my driveway where the bus stop happened to be. I stuck out like a goose in the hen house. I was a full head taller than the rest of the kids and my dark eyes were as somber and serious as a baleful poet's. I knew I was different on the outside and different on the inside. I knew that my parents were average-sized people, if not small. People that size just didn't have giant children like me. Wherever I went, from the very beginning, my incongruous size reminded me that I was put up for adoption by the mother who bore and the father who sired me.

To me, and to everyone I suppose, that meant that when I was born I was given away. Really, there is no greater repudiation than to be born and then immediately turned over to the state for redistribution. When the stainless-steel scissors severed the umbilical cord that connected me to my mother, the intent, for whatever reason, was that it would be the last physical contact with her that I would ever have. I would never know her face, her touch, or the sound of her voice . . . and she would never know mine.

It's not that I was an orphan. I had parents, good ones. It's just that as I grew up, many of the threads of my being were disconnected. My appearance, even much of my behavior, was inexplicable, because I didn't know where it came from. I couldn't say that my legs were slightly bowed, just like my dad's, or that the solemn scowl that crept onto my face during moments of solitude was from my mother's side. I had no idea where the parts, and therefore the whole, of me had come from.

In truth, these things were really too much to think about at that age. Instead, I would tell anyone who asked that my parents were my parents, the only ones I had, the only ones I ever would have. That was on the surface. Underneath, something more powerful was at work.

Three

My mother had difficulties in her first pregnancy. My sister was born this side of a miscarriage and only conceived after careful medical consultation. After that, my parents were told that if they wanted more children they should adopt. I'm sure they coped with that news the same way I've seen them cope with every turn in life: with the resolve to look at what they had instead of what they didn't. They had a healthy daughter. They had each other. And they had the ability to adopt a baby boy.

In the early sixties, adoption wasn't as difficult a proposition as it is today. In fact, there was a surplus of babies. My father, who designed computer programs, worked for General Electric. In the spirit of corporate philanthropy, GE initiated a program to encourage employees to adopt the unwanted children of the world. My parents stepped right up and became one of the first sets of adoptive parents in the program. The spate of illegitimate children at that time meant my parents were not only able to get their hands on me in a very short period of time, they were also able to adopt my brother only three years later.

I distinctly remember the day Kyle joined our family. I also remember having my parents explain to me that we were adopting him in the same way I had been adopted. Because we were adopted, I was to understand that we were special. I was only three, but I can see in my mind the city offices of the adoption agency, a dirty, yellow brick building draped with forbidding wrought-iron fire escapes. It didn't seem like a place special children would come from.

It was a cold winter day and gravel-stained piles of snow surrounded the back lot where we parked. We sat in a waiting room that wasn't unlike a doctor's office. The magnitude of the moment, however, didn't allow for playing. Besides, there were no toys like there were at the doctor's. Instead, I sat quietly kicking my shoes together. After a while, a woman emerged with a blond baby wrapped in a nappy, white baby's blanket.

"This is your brother," my mother explained to me, taking him from the nurse and tilting him up so that I could see. His eyes were shut tight, but he moved in a way that let me know he was awake.

"His parents can't take care of him," my mother explained quietly, and not for the first time. "So we're going to be his mommy and daddy."

"Like me," I said with a firm nod.

"Yes," my mother said fondly, "you were adopted, too. That's right."

I stared at my mother then, afraid to ask, but needing to say something. In the voice of the three-year-old that I was, I quietly said, "Where are his mommy and daddy?"

If there was an answer for that question, I can't say that I remember it.

It didn't take long for my brother Kyle to become the source of great consternation. Unlike my tendency toward compliance, my brother seemed possessed by a renegade spirit. At the respective ages of seven and four, I was still afraid to take an extra cookie from the jar, while my brother was already playing with matches. Kyle and I seemed to share nothing beyond a bedroom and our last name. We seemed to make an exemplary case for the power of genetics. Still, we were very close. Kyle had a mean streak that he would turn loose in a snap if anyone in the neighborhood gave me grief. It didn't matter that he was three years my junior. Even the older kids knew that while they might be twice his size, he was just as apt to pick up a garden tool and rap them with it as he was to lay into them with his teeth. And I'm ashamed to say that from time to time as we got older I would even take advantage of Kyle's fearlessness and his devotion to me by getting him to steal an occasional pocketknife from the big merchandise store nearby.

For my part, I did my best to console Kyle during his unending hours of punishment when he was relegated to our room. Once, and quite uncharacteristically, I even burst into the bathroom where he was receiving a sound spanking from my mother for biting one of the neighborhood kids.

"Let him go!" I cried, right in the face of my mother's ire.

She was more surprised than I was, and she actually stopped. I'd like to say there were numerous other occasions when I stepped in to save Kyle from the circumstances he created, but there weren't that many. He seemed destined to cross paths with trouble, over and over again. My best and most consistent efforts to help were in the area of advice, which he never took. And so, growing up, he was always a much greater asset to me than I was to him. In truth, at times I was his scourge. It was impossible for teachers, neighbors, and parents to help themselves from carelessly comparing Kyle to me. Incredibly, while most people in his situation would have despised their older brother, Kyle only seemed to love me more.

Later on, when we were teenagers, he would grudgingly accept my counsel on behavior, only to discard it the moment he left the room. It frustrated me no end to explain to Kyle that he had simply to follow the rules, only to see him go his own way time after time. To me, life was like a scout troop. The aim was to earn badges and advance. The higher you elevated yourself, the more people admired you and the easier it was for them to love you. In scouts, the way to earn badges was set out for you in the guidebook. What could be easier?

In life, I had no book, but I did have my parents. They were like the scout leaders of my life. They helped me interpret the rules and requirements along the way, advising but never pushing me to reach the next rank. They led by example. They took pride in their own hard work, and there was damn little fooling around. My dad never took a day off from work. He never even sneaked out early on a nice summer day to play golf. Same way for my mom. She didn't care if she did get five sick days a year, she worked whether she was sick or not. She had so many sick days accumulated during her teaching career that when the union negotiated a deal where teachers could cash them in, I think she had enough to buy a new car.

And if my parents were like scout leaders, then it's fair to say that I viewed our home as a scout den. It was kept in shipshape. My mother worked to make our house the envy of anyone who aspired to good housekeeping. Every meal was an event. My mom would put together breakfasts that could shame a good truck stop; clean up; shuffle my older sister, my younger brother, and me off to school; launch my dad; then make her own way to work. When she got home, she'd clean, every day. Then she'd bake. Then she'd cook dinner. Every meal hit on all four food groups, just the way they taught us in school. Only when dinner was cleaned up, the next day's lunches were fixed and bagged, and her schoolwork was complete would my mother sit back in her chair and relax with a book.

In kindergarten, it only took me one report card to realize the magnitude of those wonderful grids of letters and words. Tie your shoes, get an A. Display good manners, another A. Show consideration for classmates, bingo. If you filled that thing with A's, teachers said you were a good kid. Parents' eyes twinkled. Grandparents cooed. Aunts and uncles pursed their lips and nodded with approval. Later, shoelaces, consideration, and manners would become biology, math, and English, but it was all the same thing to me.

I wanted to be the best. I was obsessed. In school, I couldn't waste too much time fooling around with classmates. I had to listen. One missed fact could mean the difference between an A and an A–. In sports, if reckless abandon was required, I could do that, too. If it didn't come naturally, I could learn it. If I was reading a book, I lived in the world of that book.

Before I reached the age of seven, my parents had my hearing tested. My hearing, the doctors said, was fine. My level of concentration was so acute that spoken words simply couldn't break the trance I was in while reading a book.

Not all the merit badges were the sole result of hard work. That just isn't true. Whoever was responsible for my existence had left behind some good physical tools for athletics and a halfway decent mental aptitude for school. I didn't think of that then, though. I only thought about what goals would most impress my parents and the adults around me and how I could possibly achieve them.

While my inordinate drive began to pay off in obvious ways, it came at a price. At only eight years of age, I was plagued by agonizing nightmares and insomnia, the kinds of disorders more closely associated with disturbed adults. My parents would find me sleepwalking, wandering through the house, late into the night. I became terrified of sleep. I complained a little, but not much. Complaining wasn't acceptable unless, in my mother's words, your leg was cut off.

So I'd pull the covers over my head at night, even if it was warm, and hide, dreading the coming of sleep and the terror it brought. It wasn't unusual for this involuntary struggle against sleep to rage on until the room began to grow light with the dawn. I remember consoling myself during these times with the notion that this haunting could not last forever. The potency of these dreams was such that I could envision them going on for some time, but I promised myself that at least by the time I was ten, I would be able to sleep like a normal child. It had to be that way. By then, I reasoned, I wouldn't be afraid of so many things, even nightmares. I never considered their source. I wasn't that sophisticated. I had no idea then that the uncertain circumstances of my birth and my driving need to avoid any recurrence of that painful rejection fueled these nightmares. I only hoped that they might one day magically go away.

The nightmares varied, but they all had the same theme of impossibility. I was somewhere on the edge of a wintry forest, for example, and I had to get to somewhere else. This forest was as thick as an overgrown apple orchard. The crystal-white branches of the dormant trees stretched in every conceivable direction, an impermeable web. What I had to do in that dream was take my father's green station wagon through the labyrinth, and I had to do it without getting a single scratch on the car. Behind me was the abyss of hell, waiting to swallow me.

My only choice was to go forward through the trees. The impossibility of it would leave me paralyzed and moaning in agony. My mind would spin like a man trapped in a revolving door, never allowing me to go forward, never allowing me to go back. While the need to go forward was absolute, the certainty of failure was complete.

I could never extricate myself from these subconscious labyrinths alone. Shaking me awake wasn't enough. My parents would often have to put me in the bath or get me to eat something in order to pull me completely free from the dreams and my pathetic sobbing. At first, they tried to put me right back to bed, but unless I was completely free, the whole cycle would begin again. The nightmares would continue to gnaw away.

I can only compare the horror of these dreams to the insane ravings of a fever. Once in college, during a bout with the flu, my temperature rose beyond 103. In three days' time I lost twenty-three pounds. During that time, the sickness that ate away at my body and my brain approached only a fraction of the dread I felt on so many nights during my early childhood. Later, I would compare them to hell, not the hell of fire and brimstone, but the hell people describe when they talk about the complete absence of God. That was what those dreams were to me: the total absence of anything loving or forgiving or good.

At the time, I had no idea what was happening or why. I suppose now those dreams represented my yearning for control, to direct my life against the impossible odds stacked against me: the odds of becoming a football player, the odds of becoming a writer, and the unspeakable odds of becoming both. Yet as unattainable as these things seemed, my need for them was as absolute as my need to drive through the frozen forest. In my subconscious, I must have believed that if I could accomplish these things, I would not only be worthy of my own parents, I would be able to confront the parents who'd given me up.

I looked at the whole issue of success like it was some kind of business deal. With my parents, I felt pretty sure I knew what kind of achievements it would take to lock them in. In my subconscious, I knew there was no telling what it would take to please my biological parents. With a mantle of extraordinary accomplishments, however, I could confront them with confidence. I could convince them not with words but by the deeds I had done that they had made a mistake. They never should have let me go. This was the fuel that burned in the engine beneath my surface.

Four

I learned to read full-length books about the same time I started admiring football players. I had been reading for a few months—at no great rate—when my mother returned one evening from a PTA meeting. I was pulled away from the TV set and marched upstairs to get ready for bed. As I brushed my teeth in the bathroom mirror, my mother stood there in the doorway.

"I was talking with Mrs. Moorsehead tonight," she said in an offhand way that confused me. I wasn't used to having subtle hints dropped by my mother. She was typically full-steam ahead and tossed suggestions at you like medicine balls.

"She told me that Michael likes to read so much that she caught him with a flashlight and a book under his covers after she'd put him to bed. Imagine that? He likes to read so much that he even sneaks . . . "

Her admiration for my friend's transgression was obvious even to me. It was an unusual contradiction. Strict discipline and rigid adherence to all rules normally delighted my mother.

"It's really something that a boy likes to read so much," she continued, nearly winking at me. "Reading is so important."

Enough said. Before I went to bed that very night, I scampered downstairs on some lame excuse and spirited a flashlight from the tool drawer to my bed in the baggy leg of my flannel pajamas.

It fit my mother's profile as an avid reader herself, but even more so as a schoolteacher, that she would encourage me to read. It fit my profile to throw myself enthusiastically into anything bearing even the most remote possibility of praise. Having my name brought up and bragged on at the next PTA meeting meant more to me than a month full of free ice cream. There were few idle moments after that when I didn't have a book in hand. While I was going through the motions of reading at every opportunity, I became spellbound by books. This made me even more determined to someday write them. Think of the things my mother could say to Mrs. Moorsehead and the rest of the PTA ladies then!

I never imagined that a book could bring me any grief, but the fragile substructure beneath my emotions made it possible. One summer night, under the safety of my covers, I finished *Charlotte's Web*. The horror of her death caved me in. I bawled outrageously. I was so sad and so alone that I broke all the rules and walked in a catatonic state down the stairs to find my parents.

They were on the covered patio behind our house, sitting and enjoying the last wan light of the evening. When they saw me standing there in my rumpled pajamas, sobbing hysterically, my mother looked instinctively to make sure I had both legs. Until I spoke, she presumed it was just another nightmare.

"She's dead!" I wailed.

"Who?" My mother demanded in alarm. "Who's dead?"

"Charlotte," I sobbed. "It's not fair, Mom. It's not fair. Why did she have to die? Why?"

I think my parents were embarrassed for me. They shot looks between themselves and rolled their eyes. I was a hopeless baby. Here I was, a big strong growing boy with straight A's in school and promise on the athletic fields, but soft beyond comprehension. They marched me back upstairs with stern orders to get to sleep. Charlotte was a spider in a book. That didn't merit this degree of distress.

At the time I was adopted, there was a syndicated cartoon in the newspaper about a quivering basset hound who was afraid of his own shadow. The cartoon was called *Timidthy*, and my mother was mortified that people would take to calling me that since it fit so well. As my mother put me back to bed that night, I'm sure she kicked herself again for bestowing me with such an appropriate but dangerous name. In fact, I heard her clucking her tongue to herself as she made her way back down the stairs.

"You don't understand," I sobbed, cowering alone under the covers and unable to stop my crying. "You . . . don't . . . understand."

In all honesty, I didn't understand myself. Being sad is one thing, hysterics are quite another. But the thing that bothered me about Charlotte's death more than anything were the little babies she left behind. Charlotte was a beautiful creature. I loved Charlotte. Her children would never know her, and it was that fact that made me hysterical. At that time, I had no way of knowing why.

At the age of ten, I recollected the promise I'd made to myself at eight. The nightmares, although not gone, had diminished in their frequency if not in their intensity. I was like an epileptic. If too much time passed without an incident, it only made me know that one was imminent. The only thing I didn't know was how or when. Possibly part of the reason the nightmares were less frequent was that I had begun to believe I was a football player. There were signs, albeit faint, that gave me hope of acquiring that badge of honor. My coach for all three years in Little League was a man named Ron Kelly. He had played college football as well as a couple of years of semipro. He knew the game, and he believed in me. That year, when he was handing out the championship trophies to us at the league's year-ending banquet, Mr. Kelly announced to the crowd of kids and parents that I was going to be his ticket to the Rose Bowl. As I loped across the stage to accept my trophy, I blushed and inclined my head away from the school cafeteria, overflowing with young players and their parents. But even as I blushed, my mind was boiling with ideas of how I could make that happen, how I could really get to the Rose Bowl to give life to his prophecy.

My sister was fifteen at the time and in high school. The star of our community's high school football team was Pete Holohan, a neighborhood boy. He was the quarterback, and already the word on the street was that college scouts could be spotted at high school games assessing Holohan's skills. He was only a sophomore. Our high school, Liverpool, boasted about four thousand students. So for a sophomore, just making the varsity team was a milestone, let alone being a star worthy of the attention of college scouts. What I wanted to know was where had Holohan been as a freshman.

"He played on the freshman team," my sister told me, proud to be the source of important local lore. We were at the dinner table, and I considered her answer over a few mouthfuls of mashed potatoes.

"Has anyone ever played varsity as a freshman?" I inquired politely.

"No," my sister said with disdain. "Nobody could do that. If anyone could have, it would have been him."

More potatoes and a chunk of flank steak. This spurred me on. The very fact that something was unlikely meant that the rewards of admiration would be that much greater.

After a big gulp of milk, I announced, "I'm going to make the varsity team when I'm a freshman."

My sister grinned from behind her own glass of milk. I looked around the table. My mom was working on her steak in a businesslike manner, but I knew from her facial expression that my words had registered. My brother was using the distraction as an opportunity to hide his peas in his napkin. My father returned my gaze with a smile that was warmer than my sister's smirk, but just as dubious. I waited for him to speak.

"That's a nice thing to try for," he told me.

"I'm going to," I said. "I'm not just trying. I'm going to."

"No one's done it," my sister reminded me with a sniff.

"I will."

"Just don't be upset if it doesn't happen," my father said. "It's nice to try to do things, but if they don't work out . . . Well, that's okay, too."

That, I knew, was my father's credo. There would come a day when he would actually start to believe the crazy things I'd come up with, but back then he was just trying to prepare me for life's inevitable disappointments.

One of the problems that came along with trying to be Mr. Everything at the age of ten was that most of the kids around me couldn't relate to it. I developed the reputation of being a teacher's pet, always raising my hand to answer questions and getting to be captain of the kickball team in gym class more times than not. The fact that I didn't seem to care what my peers thought isolated me all the more. But as they say in love, and this is also true in friendship: Every pot has a cover.

My childhood cover—and my best friend to this day—was Stu Lisson. Stu was like the older brother I never had. He was actually a young art teacher at my elementary school. My mom taught there as well, and I got to know Stu as much through his friendship with my parents as from his being my art teacher. Whether it was because of his relationship with my mom and dad or because he considered me a singular child, Stu took me under his wing. He and Colleen (the girlfriend who later became his wife) took me to baseball games and movies. On hot summer nights, we went to Friendly's, the local ice cream place. Stu encouraged me to draw and write and become an amateur photographer. He and Colleen would take me to parks and on nature walks through the woods. They taught me to look not just at the sky, but to closely examine the bark of a tree, the shape of an anthill, or to be aware of the breeze blowing through the fine hair on the back of my arm.

My friendship with Stu did nothing to ameliorate the strangeness with which I was perceived by the other kids in school. Try as he might, his favoritism toward me in the art room was obvious and only reinforced their notion that I was a big, spoiled brownnose. It's not that I didn't have any friends—there were kids in the neighbor-hood I played with after school—but there was something that kept me just out of reach. I don't know if it was because of me or their perception of me. If there was a birthday party at the amusement park, though, I was often the one not invited. When someone had a sleepover, I'd more often than not hear about it the day after.

I was okay with that. Despite the undercurrents of discomfort with myself and my peers, I would have given my early childhood a solid eight out of ten on the happiness scale. After all, I was pleasing my parents and that was my main concern. My grades continued to be good, and I was an exemplary Cub Scout. Besides earning the praise of my football coach, I won enough medals at the yearly troop Olympics so that I got my picture in the local paper as well as a special plaque of recognition from the troop leader. And I was careful enough so that the times I did get into trouble, I didn't get caught. To me, these things, not birthday parties, were what was important.

My quest for universal adult approval and admiration was proceeding nicely. I was racing downhill with the glee of a novice skier before he is required to come to a sudden stop. Then, right before I turned twelve, I crashed. Like so many of us, I was bushwhacked by puberty. Before that time, my only concern had been to please my parents. Acceptance in my mind was measured only by adult approval. Now my body was demanding that I please my peers, most especially the girls. I thought constantly about girls and sex. I couldn't help myself. I suddenly felt a prodigious need to be cool. At the same time, I was cruelly burdened with thick glasses, unthinkable acne, and a barbarous growth spurt that somehow left the size of my face too small for its accouterments: my eyes, nose, ears, and teeth. I was even bigger proportionally to my peers than I'd been before, and now twice as awkward.

I think the best way to describe me at that time would be "pitiful." My rejection at birth was now only a dull ache that I had carefully masked. Because I never allowed myself to consciously consider my adoption, I only recognized the symptoms of distress, not the disease. But at twelve, I felt the screaming sting of immediate and palpable rejection. The girls whom I most admired sneered at me. The guys who were the coolest made fun of my clothes, glasses, and bookish willingness to please the teachers, whom they considered to be the enemy. All my accomplishments suddenly worked against me. Sports weren't cool, and neither were good grades. Boy Scouts were for worms.

There were many times during these middle school days when my loneliness became so acute that I began to seriously consider the most painless way to end my life. No one ever suspected this. I was too ashamed to talk about it. Who, after all, could admire a suicidal teenager? Outwardly, everything was fine. My engine continued to burn. I was pleasing my parents with good grades and athletic accomplishments, but living as a scourge among so many important teenage girls was so detestable to me that I might have taken action except for the fact that I was even more afraid of dying than I was of some pretty girl snickering at the carbuncle on the bridge of my nose. As painful as life was, if dying meant the possibility of living in the eternal whirlpool of my horrible night dreams, I wanted no part of it.

Five

During these loathsome times, I was in a constant state of pandering. As in every school, there was a group of kids in my middle school
who were very cool. The guys weren't particularly athletic, nor particularly smart. Likewise with the girls. They were, however, the "in"
crowd. They were the kids the rest of us wanted to be. They wore
stylish clothes without trying to be in style. Their faces had been
spared the invasion of oozing blotches or the bright red carbuncles
that tormented others. The girls were alluring and the guys were considered cute. They smoked pot. They talked back. They dated among
themselves and played outrageous games of spin the bottle. There
wasn't a single one of them who hadn't been kissed. The rest of us
looked on like the people outside the velvet ropes at the Academy
Awards, ogling and wishing.

You can imagine how far I was outside those lines. I wouldn't
smoke because it was wrong and it made me choke. I was still striving
to please teachers because I wanted good grades. I read books. The
girls weren't interested. Still, it became my personal mission to get to
the other side of that velvet. If I could only get one of those girls, I
would be "in." It didn't have to be a girl to get me there, either. If one
of the cool guys liked you, he could be a sponsor of sorts. Then the
cool girls would know you were okay, and maybe, just maybe, one of
them would agree to be your girlfriend.

I tried to comb my hair the right way, blow-drying it and fussing in front of the bathroom mirror for twenty minutes every day before breakfast. I tried to wear my clothes, made by the wrong companies and purchased at the wrong stores, in a way that most closely resembled what was really cool. I would actually lay awake at night thinking of nice things I could say to the people who counted, the guys as well as the girls. I made the mistake of thinking that if I fawned hard enough, someone would let me in.

Nothing worked. I was shamed and embarrassed at every turn. When I finally worked up the courage and gall to tell Deana Hammond, the prettiest and most developed girl in the sixth grade, that I liked her, she sneered and told me I was a creep. I walked through the rest of the school day red-faced and numb, and I pulled an unspeakable C on a social studies test. When I gathered the nerve to try and sit down at the long lunch table where all the coolest guys sat, the smallest one of the bunch told me that the three empty seats were already taken. I sat at the next table over and tried not to notice that those same seats remained empty throughout lunch.

Death seemed imminent, but instead of pushing myself through middle school like a lone man trying to move a boxcar, I hitched up to a rickety train of fellow uncool people and bumped my way down the tracks toward high school. Dan Webb and Matt Van Dugen became my closest friends. Dan was the runt of our class, but funny beyond reason. He, like me, wore glasses and dreamed about the other side of the velvet rope. Matt was less ambitious. He was white but had the large Afro of a black man. Other than his hair, he was singularly unremarkable and seemed relatively content with his place in the hierarchy of our school, as well as genuinely glad to be our friend. Both Dan and I would have sold the other two down the river for even a week at the lunch table where the cool people sat, because, as much as anything, your status was determined by your lunch table.

Not far into the sixth grade, the three of us banded together at a linoleum-clad table not far from where the cool people sat. In fact, our table became a kind of jumping-off point for people who were about to be accepted by the cool kids. Those who had been recently banished also sat there. We were the ultimate wannabes. With this kind of company, I actually began to smell the possibility of success.

Of course, we were all great pretenders. We laughed at the way Eric Jefferson's hair stood up or the way Kim Reniery had obviously stuffed her bra. We snickered at the way Denise D'Marko was being deceived by Kyle Kissell. She thought he loved her. We all knew he had a thing for Debbie Manavicci, her so-called friend. In that way, we clung to our fragile adolescent sanity.

Dan and Matt and I lived in the same suburban neighborhood, each within a half mile of the others' houses. We started hanging out together almost every day after school. In the winter, we threw snowballs at cars and hitched onto the bumpers of buses. In the spring, we stole gum and cigarettes that we pretended to smoke behind Bayberry Plaza in the jungle of weeds. Summer was spent mostly in my backyard in our pool. At night, we camped out on each other's lawns whenever we could convince our mothers to allow us to set up a tent. During the fall, we committed daring acts of vandalism, egging houses and lighting neighbors' shrubbery on fire with cans of lighter fluid. Other boys would join us from time to time, falling in and out of our ranks like mercenary soldiers. Occasionally, if the summer heat was thick enough, I could lure some opportunistic cool person into our company for an afternoon swim. But for the most part, it was the three of us.

All the while, Dan and I never stopped plotting in secret to free ourselves from Matt and each other's company. The two of us needed to be cool. All the joys of childhood were lost on us in those days. Happiness depended entirely on acceptance. In the spring of seventh grade, I finally got my chance. I had inexplicably smitten Kim Reniery, who at the time was the best friend of the most popular girl in our class. Entree ensued. I left my two friends and their lunch table without so much as a shrug.

It only took two weeks for Kim to see the error of her ways. I showed up at a Friday night dance with a planet-sized zit on my cheek. We held hands anyway, but when she wanted to dance, I was so self-conscious about sticking out in the crowd that after three minutes of dangling my limbs like a fool, I excused myself and hid in the bleachers. She broke up with me via note on Monday. It was delivered in the hallway between classes by one of her friends. I was bereaved. I entered the lunchroom with great trepidation. As unob-trusively as possible, I slid into a seat at the end of the long table. Silence ensued. I concentrated on opening my milk and meticulously unwrapped a sandwich from my bag. With shaking hands, I took a bite of ham and cheese. Finally, I had to look up. The same runt who'd denied me a year before seemed to take special delight in telling me that the seat I was in had already been taken. His mali-cious smile and the silent countenances of the others told me I was banished.

Without a word, I repacked my sandwich and made for the next table down the row. I was welcomed by disbelieving stares and si-lence. Dan was in charge there now, sitting at the head of the table like a patriarch. He smugly informed me that the empty seats at his table had been spoken for as well. I looked to Matt for help, but he wasn't the type to rock the boat. I nodded my head and began searching the busy lunchroom for someplace to sit, trying to assume a posture that suggested I had no intention of sitting with Dan any-way. Carrying my bag and my open carton of milk, I wandered through the throng of kids. In one hour, I had gone from the highest height to the lowest depth. Once again, my loneliness felt complete.

While my final conversation with Audry was the first time I fully considered my adoption, she wasn't the first person I was close to who tried to broach that subject. Kyle, my brother, and I never talked about it, nor did my parents, nor did my friend Stu. People close to me knew I lived by an unwritten rule not to discuss my beginnings. It was Matt, who remained friends with me despite my shameful fall in our school's social order, who broke that rule.

Good soul that he was, Matt never resented my apostasy, and we remained friends despite the smear campaign Dan mounted against me—until one night that summer. Matt was also adopted, a fellow space traveler cast adrift in a universe of deep emotional uncertainty. We never talked about it, though, and that's the way I liked it. It had nothing to do with our friendship, or so I believed. It was mere coin-cidence. The only reason I even knew he was adopted was that my mom told me one day when she was remarking what a nice boy Matt was.

"He's adopted too, you know," she told me enthusiastically. I think she was submitting this as further evidence that adopted children could be good despite the questions being raised in my own household at the time. Kyle hadn't mended his ways in the least. If anything, he was more off course than ever. His grades were beginning to sag precipitously and his undisciplined behavior was extremely disconcerting to my mother, since he was still a student at the elementary school where she taught.

Matt and I, however, were proof positive to my parents that there was hope for adopted kids despite my younger brother's problems. Then one night, Matt and I were sleeping out in his backyard, talking about the girls we would like to sleep with and the boys we would like to beat within inches of their lives, when he broke the unwritten rule between us. I don't know if he knew I even had a rule or not, but for me to be friends with a kid who had experienced the same kind of abandonment I had was dangerous. It naturally conjured up questions and begged for comparisons. Matt and I had known each other for a couple of years, and I simply expected he knew better than to bring up anything too close to home.

It was a sultry night. Crickets sang beyond the orange luminescence of the tent's walls. The grass had already begun to sweat dew. The air inside our enclave was moist and hot. We had tied back the nylon flaps on the window and the triangular entrance. We lay on the top of our musty sleeping bags wearing nothing but underwear. Beyond the screen an unearthly glow from the streetlight draped Matt's single-story house in a halo. Mosquitoes bumped quietly against the synthetic screens.

"Hey, Tim," he said in the midst of the quiet, as if he was about to say something he had been considering for a long while, "did you ever wonder about your parents?"

"My parents are probably sleeping right now," I replied flippantly. "Or checking on my brother. He's been getting on the roof and shooting at people's windows with my BB gun. They hide the gun, but he can find anything."

"No," he said, "I don't mean *them*."

We both fell silent. To me it was as if we were two soldiers stalking the jungles of Vietnam. Matt had just tripped a wire, and we were in that horrible moment, waiting for the explosion that would rip us open from the belly button down, the way some savage biker might tear the top off a beer can. That's what it would have done to me if I stayed there. Talking about the mother who gave me up would have ripped me open. But I wasn't going that way. I jumped sideways, springing heroically off the trail, saving myself. Unfortunately, the explosion of that remark ripped my friend to pieces. While I could save myself, the very fact that Matt, adopted himself, had broached the subject made him as good as dead to me.

"I don't have any other parents," I hissed maliciously, as if I were spitting on his mangled corpse, hating him for tripping the wire, for bringing me so close to my own destruction, for, as far as our friendship went, destroying himself.

I rolled up my sleeping bag and stuffed it into my big canvas backpack along with my musty clothes. I pulled on my gym shorts and shouldered the pack before scrambling out of the tent and into the muggy night. Matt's body never moved, and he never spoke. I think he realized what happened and knew it was too late to do anything about it. By the time I trekked through a half mile of backyards to my own home, the dewy grass had stained my feet lime green. The door was never locked. An agitated complaint escaped from the hinges as I let myself in. I crept upstairs past my parents' bedroom door. It was shut tight, but I knew they were there and I knew I was now safe, at least for the time being.

Six

Mercifully, football rescued me from the angst of early adolescence. I had outgrown the weight limits of Little League football and would have had to sit out a year from the sport but for a new program that was being initiated in the school system. In recognition of the fact that some kids develop earlier than others, the high school athletic director opened up the freshman sports teams to qualifying eighth graders. All I needed was to pass a doctor's physical, take a fitness test, and get permission from my parents.

When eighth grade began, I no longer cared about what the kids around me thought. I didn't care where I sat at lunch or which girls liked me. I spent my afternoons on one of the high school football fields, with the biggest, strongest, toughest high school freshmen. They were the ones I now wanted to like me. They were the ones whose parties I wanted invitations to. All that happened and more. Although I was a year younger, I was the biggest of the bunch, and I dominated the football field as if I were two years their senior. Off the field, I was quiet and deferential to my freshman teammates, and therefore accepted. They taught me how to drink beer and introduced me to girls who were willing to do things I had only dreamed of.

I floated through my last year of middle school aloof from my peers, thinking and acting like a high school student. I worked hard in school, without worrying what people thought when I raised my hand. I stopped trying to be nice in the hallway. I stopped fretting over my clothes and my hair. In a way, I was more alone than ever before, but that was okay. At least I was free from the pandering and worrying about the approval of my peers. I could now focus completely on worrying about perpetuating the small achievements that I had already made. In the back of my mind, I could hear the whisper of the statement I'd made about varsity football at the dinner table when I was ten.

On a rainy fall day, we played our final freshman game. A howling wind churned the gray and white sky. A nip was in the air, but we were too honored by the presence of George O'Leary, the varsity coach, to notice the chill. He'd come to see if there were any of next year's sophomore class that merited consideration for the varsity. The freshman coach told me on the side that he was also coming to see me. I played that game with an anger and a viciousness that impressed even Coach O'Leary. All the suffering I'd done over the past two years, all the hurt I had stored away during my first thirteen years, I was somehow able to bring to the surface in that game. When I had a shot at the quarterback, I didn't just tackle him, I rammed my helmet through his ear hole, knocking him out of the game. When I was blocking on offense, I didn't just block my man at the line, I'd dispose of him and then go downfield into the defensive secondary looking for more people to savage.

Throughout my football career, it was the turmoil inside that enabled me to play the game with remarkable ferocity. The questions I had about who I was, the anger at being cast aside, and the determination to prove I was worthy—all negative things—became assets on the football field. We all have a dark side, but in football the anger and violence generated by that dark side are not only acceptable, they give you an edge. You're supposed to be mean. Bad is good. Instead of consuming your psyche from within, football encourages, even celebrates, the expulsion of these malevolent emotions.

I began to feed off of my own pain as well as the pain I was causing in others. When you get to that point in a game of football, it's like that first moment behind the wheel of a car when you punch down the accelerator on a wide-open ribbon of road. The feeling is pure. I began to chortle to myself upon impact. In the huddle, while the rest of my teammates sucked for air, I grinned uncontrollably. Drool ran unchecked from the corners of my mouth.

By the end of that game, my own teammates were afraid of what I might do. I acted crazy, especially when it was over. As high as I was during the contest was as low as I was when we lost. I began to sob hysterically on the sideline right in full view of the most important man in my life. It was as if the defeat belonged to me personally. My dream of leading our team to victory and stamping an indelible impression on the mind of George O'Leary was lost. And because I had slipped and shown my true character in full view of the coach, the intensity of my crying doubled. I knew that gruff-looking Irishman, standing there with his weathered red face in a light wind-breaker and shorts, impervious to the weather, would never make a crybaby the first freshman ever to play on the varsity.

After football, I started to wrestle, again for the freshman team. That kept me mentally removed from my middle school peers. Before I knew it, spring arrived. It wasn't the crying, but the intensity of emotion that generated my effort in that final football game that prompted Coach O'Leary to ask the middle school phys ed teacher to see if I had any interest in lifting weights at the high school that spring. My hopes were renewed. Dave Pittard, an assistant varsity football coach who also coached lacrosse, drove past the middle school every day on his way to practice at the high school. Without ever speaking to me directly, Coach O'Leary arranged for Coach Pittard to pick me up three days a week during the last hour of school. The last hour at the middle school was the activities period where people participated in everything from sewing to chess. Coach O'Leary convinced my principal that it would be advantageous for me to have weight lifting as my activity.

The weights were in an old storage room that Coach O'Leary had confiscated upon his arrival from Long Island, where he'd built a series of championship teams. He was brought to Liverpool to restore its football team to former days of glory, so no one complained when he cleared out the room and had its cinder block walls painted over. He also demanded that the booster club give him the money to buy some rusty old Universal weight machines and about five thousand pounds worth of free weights from a bankrupt health club. When I first entered that room, Coach O'Leary wouldn't even look at me, but I saw him direct an assistant my way to tell me what was expected. Chalk dust swirled in the air amid punctuated grunts and shouting.

In the hubbub of that busy weight room, I was completely alone. Not one of my teammates from the freshman team had been asked to attend these lifting sessions. I was working out with the prospective varsity team. These were young *men*, shaving, driving cars, talking carelessly about drinking and sex. At first, no one spoke to me. I moved between stations, waiting quietly for machines to open up before I pumped out my exercises and checked them off on my card. But as the spring wore on, I got stronger, and the older players became accustomed to my presence. While some certainly resented my encroachment on their turf, others begrudgingly began to afford me respect.

At the end of every week, in the middle of Friday's session, Coach O'Leary would get up on a bench in the middle of the weight room and hand out two Liverpool Football T-shirts to the players he thought had worked the hardest that week. As you can imagine, I spent a lot of time laying awake nights thinking about how to get one of those shirts. I lifted and stretched. I tortured my body to its limits in the quest for a shirt. Finally, two weeks before school was to let out for the summer, Coach O'Leary paid me some attention. At the end of Wednesday's workout, I became aware of the coach standing behind me. I was doing bicep curls with a straight bar. I grunted out the last three repetitions and let the weights crash to the padded floor.

"Pick it up," the coach grunted in his Long Island accent.

My arms were rubber, but I did as he said.

"Keep going," he said disdainfully.

As the coach goaded me on, the rest of the players gathered around me in the room and began shouting and cheering for me to keep going. As I groaned the weights up toward my body, the noise grew louder and louder. After six, my head spun. I could no longer even feel my arms. They had stopped hurting at three.

"One more!" O'Leary barked.

I wobbled, shook, and twisted my back, working for every angle and using every muscle that could help the weight back up to my chest. The noise in the room was now deafening. The cheering was for me. Whether they liked me or not, the rest of them had been bitten by the contagious thrill of seeing another person push himself beyond the limits we all seem to agree are rational. With a final scream of my own, the bar banged up against my chest before falling to the mat and spilling its steel plates onto the floor. As the cheering subsided, Coach O'Leary, with what I swear was a faint smile, walked out of the room without another word.

That Friday, I got my T-shirt. The coach had to kick me out of the room that night so he could get home for dinner. As he locked up, he told me that if I had a good summer of workouts with the varsity, I would be the first freshman ever to make the team and earn a letter. He let the keys drop. They jangled against the side of his leg, clipped to his belt loop by a long cord. I was standing in the hallway, wondering if he'd said what I thought he said and waiting to be dismissed. Then he looked me full in the eye and warned me sternly that this was by no means a foregone conclusion. In fact, he said, I would most likely end up on the junior varsity squad. But, he reiterated, if I worked hard enough, there was a chance.

He had no idea he was giving me the opportunity to realize a brazen goal I had set four years before at the age of ten. That summer, I wasn't really aware of what was happening to my body, and I didn't care. All I cared about was making that team, working so hard and so long lifting weights in the weight room and running on the high school track that Coach O'Leary would have to put me on the varsity. My mornings that summer began at the Bayberry Plaza movie theater, cleaning the urine and crap off the bathroom floors and scraping gum from the backs of the theater seats. By noon, I would emerge from the cavernous theater filthy and blinking from the bright summer sun. Typically, I had the time to spend a couple of hours at home by our pool, often alone, reading books, baking in the sun, and brooding about the workouts I would attend later in the day.

One night in August, after staying in the weight room until it was time to close up and turn out the lights, I was offered a ride home by the coach. We lived in the same neighborhood, so it was no problem, he told me, to drop me off on his way. Normally, I walked the two miles from the high school to my house and didn't mind it. It gave me a chance to cool down and work some of the blood and lactic acid out of my muscles after the heavy lifting. But I wouldn't have turned down an invitation from Coach O'Leary if he asked me to dive into a pit of hot asphalt, so I bashfully accepted.

"Take a shower," he said brusquely. "I'll wait for you in my office."

After a shower, I lingered politely outside his half-open office door, too afraid to knock or say anything. When he finally noticed me, he pursed his lips and stuffed some papers into a well-worn leather briefcase. I followed him like a puppy to his wood-paneled station wagon and got into the front seat beside him. I marveled as he moved his hands and feet, operating the controls to stop for red lights and signal his turns. The coach always struck me as a man who stopped for nothing and made his intentions known to no one.

We were halfway home before he spoke. "You've worked hard."

He looked over at me for the first time. His Irish face had been burned pink by the sun. Most men, with his rosy cheeks accentuated by freckles and sandy blond hair, would have looked friendly. But it was Coach O'Leary's intention to look foreboding, and he typically wore the tough, squinty-eyed expression of a fighter.

I absorbed the compliment and wedged my hands between my bare thighs and the vinyl car seat, clenching them tight to keep myself from fidgeting. I waited like that for him to go on, but he didn't say another thing until we came to a brief halt in front of my house. He never took the car out of gear, but he did extend his strong freckled hand when he said, "I'm going to have you on the varsity. Congratulations. You earned it."

I think I mumbled my thanks. I know I shook his hand. But I glanced only briefly into his eyes before I hurried from the car. I was deathly afraid he would recant if he saw me cry.

Seven

While the influence of different men in my life—coaches, teachers, or friends—wore away at me slowly the way a stream will smooth the edges of a stone, the impact of women was sudden. One minute I was someone I thought I knew, the next, a woman would come into or go out of my life and change everything. I suppose that because my life began with such a wrenching, my interaction with women was destined to be that way.

While I may have staved off the need for social acceptance, there is no denying that I still wished I had it. What teenager doesn't want to be liked and admired by his peers? Until high school, my incongruity had been too great for that. Because of this, my confidence, as high as it was at times in the classroom and on the football field, was still nonexistent with other kids my age. I'd been with girls, but nothing more than novelty groping in darkened rooms. I wanted fiery romance with passionate lovemaking in broad daylight. However, I suspected that for a girl to be attracted to me, she would have to be first and foremost attracted to the merit badges I had acquired. Beyond that, I didn't think there was much about me that could create the kind of heat I was looking for. All that changed in one night with one girl.

After ten full days of a grueling football camp in the late summer heat, high school classes began. On the first Friday of the school year, there was an annual welcome-back dance. Before the dance there was an enormous bonfire behind the bleachers of the football field, a pep rally in honor of the new varsity team. Wooden pallets were stacked twenty feet into the air. Atop the pile, an effigy of the next week's season-opening opponent rested on a broomstick that had been planted painfully up his backside. As the fire roared, the football team joined hands with the cheerleaders and made a moving circle around the conflagration. (Later, Coach O'Leary would resoundingly berate us for dancing about publicly "like a bunch of fairies.")

Each member of the team wore his jersey to the dance, and it was a badge of honor equaled by none other. I was giddy in mine. I walked the two miles through a familiar maze of neighborhood streets and green areas by myself, thinking about the new world about to open up before me. In a school of four thousand kids, the cliques that had been established in the four area middle schools would be so diluted that there was an unavoidable reshuffling of the teenage social hierarchy. Everyone had to start over, and nothing could have pleased me more. I didn't know for certain how I would fare, but the jersey and my historical appointment to the varsity football team as a ninth grader gave me more hope than ever that social conquest and admiration among peers would be mine.

After swirling around the fire for a while like a fairy, I was bright-faced and glazed with sweat. I had been holding the hand of a uniformed cheerleader whom I knew to be a senior. At first, she gave me a doubtful look, but still she hung on. When the fire burned low and the circle began to disperse, she even managed a pleasant smile. I ducked my head, blushed, and followed the crowd into the gymnasium.

It was gloomy and loud inside. Lights shaded with green, red, and blue plastic coverings made it hard to see clearly. The band was loud and you could feel the heavy thumping bass in the spaces between your teeth. Everyone had to lean close and yell to hope for even the slightest chance of being heard. In the middle of the gym, couples danced while the rest of the throng swirled lazily around them.

My teammates stood out in their white jerseys, and many of them already had girls clinging to their arms. The rest clustered together in groups of three or four, searching the crowd for likely prey. I meandered. Even though I wore a jersey and was on the team, I seemed a breed apart from my teammates. They had arrived together in cars of their own, or ones belonging to their parents. They all knew each other from prior years. I was just a big kid whom the coach thought showed promise. I would stop and smile and try to say something to them, but we had very little in common. They were each involved in their own various stages of swooping down on a female.

Then I saw Annette. Electricity shot from my groin to the stem of my brain. I had seen titillating sights before, but only in magazines. My dad never had them, but I had plenty of friends whose fathers kept *Playboy* in their dresser drawers. I knew what a beautiful woman looked like, and this was a beautiful woman. She wasn't a high school girl. I mean, she was, but she wasn't. There wasn't a boy in that gym—or a man in the entire town, for that matter—who would have been taken by surprise to see her face and body in the pages of the magazines they kept tucked away with their underwear and socks. She was nothing less than a centerfold.

She emerged from the surrounding gloom, 5'10" with long thin legs. Her breasts, magnificently shaped, strained against the cotton fibers of a sky-blue shirt decorated with just a hint of lace around the edges of its sleeves and collar. Her eyes matched the color of the shirt, and they were as mischievous as they were felicitous. She owned the world and she knew it. Anything she wanted could be hers. Her hair spilled over her shoulders and halfway down her back, a golden mane swept carelessly away from her face. When she smiled, which she did freely, she showed all her teeth, white and perfect.

She was so beautiful that she pushed me beyond the image of the best-looking girl in the sixth grade calling me a creep. I was even ready to risk my newfound pride as a football player. I didn't know who she was or where she'd come from, but I knew I wasn't going to go through the rest of my life wishing I'd done something instead of helplessly watching her disappear into the throng. Besides, I was wearing a varsity jersey. I put myself directly into her path, and she pulled up short as if I had startled her.

"Do you want to dance?" I bellowed.

"What?" she returned above the noise, her words accompanied by a smile.

"Do you want to dance?" I yelled, encouraged by the smile and daring to lean closer to her ear.

More white teeth jumped out at me from the liquid gloom, and she shook her head no. I was smitten, but relieved at the same time. I could no sooner dance than a monkey could paint a self-portrait. Despite any athletic prowess I might have, my sense of rhythm was as nonexistent as it had been during my most awkward stage in middle school. I only asked because I couldn't think of anything else to say.

"Do you want to come with me and my friends to a party?" she said quite unexpectedly, also leaning close.

I rode crunched into the backseat of her Gremlin with another girl, listening to three of them giggle out loud about how cute I was as if I weren't there at all. To hear her call me cute made me drunk with excitement. For the first time, I realized that a summer's worth of weight lifting and sun had transformed me. I had been too preoccupied with making the varsity team to really consider my appearance, but my body was tan and fit and my face had finally caught up to my features.

Cars parked end to end suddenly lined the dark suburban street. We had to drive two blocks past the noisy party to find a spot. The low thumping bass from the sound system could be heard the moment we got out of the car, and I wondered what the neighbors were thinking. I could never imagine having a party, even if my parents were gone for the weekend, as this person's obviously were.

We walked inside through the kitchen, Annette's hand placed tentatively on my shoulder. Three steel kegs of beer rested in garbage cans that spilled ice out onto the linoleum floor. In almost every person's hand was a big, foggy plastic cup filled with beer. We moved through the crowd into the living room. They stared at us the way people do when a striking couple enters a restaurant full of diners. It was the most exciting moment of my life to date.

"I'll get us a drink," I said, feeling suave amid the shocked stares of the teammates who had witnessed my entrance.

It took a few minutes to push my way back through the kitchen and get my hands on the spigot. When I finally returned to the living room where I'd left her, she was gone. I took a good slug from my cup and began a frantic search, trying all the while to maintain my suave demeanor.

At the other end of the house was a sunken den with orange shag carpet and a large TV. The coffee table had been pushed into the corner to spare the shins of the revelers. My heart sank when I saw Annette standing in the middle of the room talking to Marco Coleman, another football player—taller, older, and more handsome than I. Her two friends quickly snuggled up beside me like mother hens and cooed for me not to worry. I was still very cute. Finally, Marco made some remark and left her side. She made her way over to the three of us.

"Thank you for the beer," she said, relieving me of the frosty cup and flashing her friends a look that dispersed them like roaches in the sunlight.

"I'm sorry," she said in a low voice, leaning toward me and surreptitiously looking around, "but my boyfriend is here. I didn't think he would be, but he is, and he wants to hang out. You understand, don't you?"

I had no idea, but nodded that I did. In my ears, I could hear a sound like ocean waves crashing down on me. She was leaving me. I wasn't enough. The whole thing was a ruse.

Then, around that perfect smile, she said, "You're sweet. How about a rain check?"

"A rain check?" I choked.

"Yeah," she said. "Another time."

"Okay," I said, nodding like a simpleton, and then she was gone.

Was she trying to make it easier for me? I was sick with shame. The cool plastic cup in my hand and the warm musty smell of the beer beckoned seductively. I knew what alcohol could do. I'd used it before. When the gnawing in my brain became too much, relief was only three or four beers away. I learned that lesson at the age of thirteen. It hadn't been uncommon for me to wander into the house on a Friday night with my teeth feeling numb, mumble to my unsuspecting parents that I was tired, and make quickly off to bed, where I would lie and spin in the painless shallows of inebriation. The bad dreams could never get me when I was drunk.

I found some older teammates in the kitchen and was happy to impress them with how much beer I could drink and how fast I could drink it. When I had enough to dull the barb of failure, I meandered back through the party to see what I could see. Annette was gone, but that didn't mean I had to be alone. I was fearless now, and my entrance with Annette legitimized me in the eyes of the girls who remained. Out of the corner of my eye I caught one with a passable face looking my way. Desperate for any small gesture of acceptance, I staggered up and asked her to go outside.

On the side lawn, we ducked behind some bushes into the streetlight's shadows. In the cool, damp grass, I fumbled inexpertly with her bra. My kisses were drunken and sloppy. I pretended that there was no difference between this girl and Annette. The alcohol enabled me to convince myself that it didn't matter, one girl was the same as the next. This girl wanted me. Annette wanted me. I wanted to bring the thrill of earlier in the night back to life. I wanted to make love with a beautiful woman. It could happen tonight. This could be it. So without being forceful, I struggled and I tried. It soon became clear that this girl was not going to allow my hands to travel any farther than the waistband of her pants. I got up off the ground and staggered into the house to see if I couldn't find a ride home.

The next morning I awoke with a monster drumming resolutely in my brain. My small bedroom, crammed with furniture, seemed more constricting than ever. It was 10:30 in the morning. On the desktop beside my bed, the phone book lay open. A page had been mangled beyond recognition, and in its midst lay one small scrap of legible names and numbers. I had obviously been afraid that in last night's state I would forget everything. One of the numbers belonged to Annette, and over the top of the scrap, written in a thick green marker that I must have found in the dark, were the barely legible words "RAIN CHECK." I could hear the words as if she were speaking to me right then.

Afraid of thinking better, I picked up the phone with trembling hands and dialed. I could see her in my mind, the tall vital form, the flashing teeth. There was a chance that she'd really meant what she'd said. A rain check: a postponement of the acceptance of an offer. She was worth even another rejection. Her father answered and sounded solemn. It made me queasy, but he got Annette anyway.

"Hi, this is Tim. From last night. Did you mean it?" I blurted out. "About the rain check?"

She giggled on the line and said, "You didn't forget? You're so cute. Yes, I meant it."

"When?" I said, hungry and anxious to sink my teeth into the opportunity before it spoiled.

"Soon, if you want," she told me.

"This week?"

"Okay, maybe Tuesday night," she said. "You call me."

On Tuesday after football practice, I called. My parents, God bless their philanthropy, were to be out that night at a charity fund-raiser. My sister had left the week before for college. I gave my brother $10 and told him to lose himself. The house was mine. She arrived in her own car, and I invited her to sit on the couch. Within five minutes, I was on top of her, unbuttoning her shirt, not knowing how far the whole thing would go, but perfectly willing to try for it all.

"We better move upstairs," she whispered. We did.

I had no idea what I was doing, but it didn't seem to matter, because she certainly did.

For three days, I did nothing in school but write her name over and over again in the blank pages of my notebooks. Under my breath, I'd whisper her name. I was ill with her. Later, I would come to find that she was a promiscuous girl. I liked to think of her as finicky. She had one boyfriend who was twenty-five and Marco, the one from the party who was a junior on the football team. Still, she was perfection, and I was sleeping with her. As a mere mortal I felt no right to reproach the behavior of a goddess.

While I came to the realization that I was her plaything, I also knew I was helpless. She would pick me up in her car and drive to some remote spot or arrange to meet me at her house when her parents were out. Word spread fast. In the locker room, the upperclassmen looked at me and pointed in bewilderment. I had gained more respect with Annette than I ever could have done by tackling quarterbacks. It wasn't just respect from my teammates that I gained; I gained respect from myself. If I could be with Annette, anything was possible. If I was attractive to her, a girl every older guy I knew dreamed of, then it had to be that I could attract other girls as well.

Like any good drug, the high I got from Annette soon wasn't enough. I wanted more, the next thing. I wanted a romance worthy of the physical inferno. I wanted Mercedes from *The Count of Monte Cristo*, I wanted Penelope from *The Odyssey*, stories I'd read where women would sooner spend their lives alone than live without the men to whom they'd given their hearts. I wanted a woman to love me like that, forever, no matter what. I wanted it. I needed it. How could I have known then the rarity of such a woman and the pain that search would cause me?

Eight

I glimpsed her in the school hallway. Her face flashed in the crowd and then she was by me, too shy to stop or slow down. I turned, followed her, desperate for her to stop, perhaps talk to someone I knew so I could later ask them all about her. I followed her all the way to her next class. The bell rang. I was late, but I didn't care. She knew I had followed her. When she got to her class, she sat down at her desk in the middle of the room. She hung her head, allowing her dark hair to drape across her blushing cheeks. I liked her more for being shy. I had learned from Annette that a brazen girl could be a dangerous poison. I stood in the doorway until I recognized a boy whose name was familiar to me.

"Can I *help* you?" the teacher demanded from behind his desk, catching me in the last seconds of my search.

"I . . . no," I said, glancing at her one more time before retreating into the halls and to my own class, where I pleasantly accepted the berating from my own teacher for coming in after the bell.

Her name was Kate. She was ashamed at the time because she had allowed another boy to kiss her. She told me that in tears one night on a coat-covered couch at a Friday night party. We had wanted to be alone, and the rest of our classmates laughed and gossiped and drank amid the loud thumping music in the house outside our enclave. I found the den where the coats were kept and where the father of the house—away to Chicago for the weekend—had an expensive stereo.

I had dialed in some soft music and it was there, on the coats, in the green light of the console, where we exchanged our first secrets.

We became inseparable. On weekends, when we weren't going to parties, we were seeing movies with Stu and Colleen. I became a fixture in her family's den, riding my bike five miles to be with her until I turned sixteen and my dad gave me his old orange Subaru coupe. Then I was there twice as much as before. I told everyone that I was going to marry Kate, and she said the same thing. She was pretty and quiet and in all the top classes at school. She was an excellent athlete. Everyone seemed to like her. As we got older, we'd find ways to spend entire nights together, each of us pretending to stay at the house of a friend.

As happy as I was to have my own Penelope, my Mercedes, there were many other things I worried over. Nightmares continued to haunt my nights and anxiety plagued my days. I shared these with Kate. It made things better. Although my grades and sports were good, it wasn't enough. When I made the All-County football team as a sophomore, I needed to make All-State. When I made All-State as a junior, I needed to become an All-American. I needed a college scholarship. I won the regional wrestling championships as a junior, but I knew I wouldn't be happy until I won the state title. With so many things going so well, no one but Kate could feel a scintilla of sympathy.

Only Kate knew me well enough to know that despite all the accomplishments, there was something inside me that would never allow any of them to be enough. To the outside world I was the golden boy who had it all. It seemed to many of my peers that, without even trying, I had all the things they wished for. They never knew that the things they presumed had swelled me with pride did little to assuage the suffering in my heart. Most people never saw me after wrestling practice, when everyone else was wearily dragging themselves to the showers. Those practices were so physically exhausting that to this day they make even my remembrances of a brutal NFL practice seem like afternoon tea. It was after these gut-wrenching sessions that I separated myself, staying late, working drills with my coach, Jack Williams, beyond the point of exhaustion, never satisfied that I'd practiced enough. I pretended I was doing those things for Kate, but it was me I was doing them for, doing them so that I would be loved, doing them so I would be worthy of that love.

Then, during the summer before my senior year in high school, I went to visit my sister in California. She had left with her boyfriend several months before, much to our parents' chagrin. Having me and my brother Kyle out to visit her was a way of making peace, letting our parents know that while she may have left the state suddenly and unexpectedly, she wasn't leaving the family. Neither Kyle nor I had been out of the state, and we'd only been on an airplane once before.

For Kyle and me, it was like being kids again. We had no one telling us what to do. I was in charge, and we both knew that meant Kyle was going to do what he damn well pleased. But I think just knowing that he was free enabled Kyle to be a simple kid brother. The people he'd begun to hang around with now that he was in high school were dubious at best, derelicts who wore denim jackets and black Def Leppard T-shirts and kept their hair long. But out there in California, he was just Kyle. He put away his juvenile delinquent regalia and wore the shorts and collared shirts my mother had purchased for both of us to take on the big trip to the land of the sun.

We went to Disneyland with my sister and her boyfriend, Frank. At seventeen and fourteen, Kyle and I were more like seven and four. We rode the rides and screamed and held our hands above our heads to really feel the pull of gravity on the roller coasters. We ate cotton candy and Sno Cones like we had to catch up on our entire child-hoods. Frank and Laurie did whatever we wanted, and we were like one big family. My sister had gotten into great shape and had a tan. I think she was happy in that California scene, and she treated the two of us like real kid brothers. We hadn't all gotten along that well since my sister had become a teenager.

During most days, Kyle and I would walk across the street from our sister's apartment either for lunch or dinner, and I'd buy $15 worth of tacos at Taco Bell. Back then, Taco Bell was only a California thing. Kyle and I had never even had a taco before, and that week we couldn't get enough. I'd get him the big Coke he always wanted at home but could never have because it was a waste of money. He got me to go out on a limb and try the hot sauce. I crave it to this day. It was a magical trip, but we should have known that it was only that eerie calm before a storm. Kyle's life was about to teeter off an unimaginable precipice, and I was about to have my heart torn out.

I spoke to Kate every day while I was gone, and except for a party that she'd gone to with her friends one night and a picnic the next day, I had a pretty good idea how she'd spent every minute without me. Upon my return, she met me at the airport with my parents. Everything looked fine. She was as pretty as ever. She smiled when she saw me. We kissed while my parents looked away, then held hands while we walked through the airport, my brother and I telling my parents about the trip in great detail. It was later, when I drove her home, that everything fell apart.

"I have to talk to you," she said nervously. "Can you stop here for a minute?"

My stomach sank. I tried hard to think of some painless reason why she would make such a request. I pulled the car into a Friendly's parking lot. I looked at her, afraid of what I saw. There was something worldly about Kate, something that hadn't been there when we'd first met, but something that had grown in her over time, not allowing me to recognize it until now. She wasn't that shy, smart, pretty little girl anymore. She was like Annette, cunning and brazen, beautiful to look at, beautiful to touch, exotic and sensual. The innocence was gone. It only made sense that she had betrayed me with Annette's old boyfriend, Marco Coleman. Home from college on vacation, he had been to the party and the picnic. He had worked his charm, exacted his revenge.

Kate told me all the things that any of us have heard when we've been let go. She said she loved me. She said she needed time, needed space, that if I let her go, only then could she know if we were meant to be. If she came back, then it was so, but only by being free from me could she know. I was sick, angry. Most of all, I was scared to death. It was happening all over again. I was being cut free, but there wasn't freedom for me. I was being rejected in a way that made me retch. I cried uncontrollably for days. I moped through school in a daze without seeing, without thinking. My parents looked on and were ill themselves, unable to fathom how their strong son could fold so quickly from the sting of forsaken love.

Every night for two weeks straight I went to Stu's. We'd watch old black-and-white movies with uplifting messages. Colleen would make us popcorn and bring us drinks, careful not to say too much, careful not to remind me too much of the kind of woman I wished I had. The three of us would sit on their couch and for a few hours I could actually forget about how sick at heart I was. After the movies, Stu and I would put on our coats, kiss Colleen good-bye on the cheek, and walk for hours through the abandoned streets of their neighborhood. We talked about life. I cried about Kate. But we never stopped walking, and slowly over those days, my best friend some-how rebuilt my spirit.

Stu sensed that I'd lost more than a high school girlfriend, but we never spoke about it specifically. He just did what he did for me all my life, what he does to this day. He bolstered me with wonderful images of how far I'd come and how far I had yet to go. He didn't talk about how I'd get over what had happened with Kate. He didn't mention the hurt. He simply drowned it in the context of the great things I had yet to do with my life. That was how Stu saw me, as a person destined for great things. And slowly I began to believe it again myself. I patched the gaping wound in my soul and began to go back to the business of making myself desirable. Kate, I reasoned, was an aberration. She had made a terrible mistake.

A good part of me was viciously angry. Then, I had no way of knowing why. Now I know that because she had cut me so deeply, because the wound was old and well-used, I had to hurt her back. Because she had rejected me, I needed to reject her. I needed to be the one to let the other go. I needed to be the one to walk away, to crush the other's spirit, to talk glibly about freedom and cast away our memories together like worthless trinkets.

I did it with cold cunning and precision. I went after every girl who approached her equal in looks, brains, and athletics. I dated the girls closest to her heart, the girls she talked disparagingly about when we had been together, the girls she feared could usurp her position as the one everyone wanted. A battle ensued. She did the same to me, dating my friends at a breakneck pace.

After thoroughly dashing me, she wanted us to be together again. Finally, I had her back. Then I cast her aside. Then I took her back, then cast her away again. Nothing she could do could make me jealous, because she was as dead to me as my childhood friend Matt. She'd crossed a line. I played with her in the cruel way a cat bats about a live, half-eaten mouse—without remorse, in fact, with pleasure. This was the depth of the wound she had reopened.

I stopped feeling for anyone outside my inner circle: my parents, my brother, Stu, my coaches, some teachers. I became a machine. I ran for president of the student government because it was an enviable accomplishment. I won in an outrageous landslide, despite the fact that my fellow seniors voted against me by a four-to-one margin. The underclassmen whisked me into office, knowing only of my accomplishments: the football player, the student, the one colleges were crawling over themselves to get to. I became the All-American. I won the state wrestling title, ripping through opponents on my way to a 36–0 record with a frightening viciousness.

Despite those accomplishments, unmatched by even the great Pete Holohan, my senior class didn't vote me most athletic. They voted me class brownie, a kiss-ass. When I got up to speak at commencement, I was booed. The truth was, these things barely hurt. I was mentally gone from that high school long before it was over. During the winter of my senior year I spent my weekends being flown around the country to colleges that wanted me to play football. When it came time to announce where I'd decided to go, the local television stations cut into their daytime programming to cover the press conference. When I announced that I'd chosen Syracuse University over the likes of Penn State, Notre Dame, and Ohio State, my picture was on the front page of the next morning's paper. They called me a hometown hero. That spring I began my summer job before school let out. I began to train at the university with my future teammates.

My college career began my freshman year at Syracuse with a two-mile run. All summer I'd trained for that run along with my weight lifting. Coach O'Leary had been hired away from Liverpool after my sophomore year. He was now the line coach at SU. It was he who had done most of the recruiting of me for Syracuse. I knew what he expected of me, and I knew his temperament. Once I was signed, I was just like any other freshman to him. That two-mile run would be the arena where I established just what kind of a player I would become.

It was training camp. My first night away from home had been unsettled. The anxieties of the upcoming day of physical tests left me unable to sleep. Despite being nervous for the upcoming events, I ate breakfast at the dining hall for energy. Still, when the whistle sounded, I raced out in front of my new teammates and held that pace as we dashed around the cones marking the outer perimeter of the field. Two smaller players soon passed me. That was all right. I knew there was no chance to beat the wiry wide receivers and defensive backs. It was in the field of big men that I felt I absolutely must finish first.

With a single lap to go, my stomach churned and vomit spilled up out of my mouth, covering the front of my sweaty T-shirt. I didn't bother to stop or even turn my head. I never even broke stride. The only thing I cared about was finishing that race first in my group. It was the way I began my college football career, it was the way I ended it: without concern for pain or discomfort or my well-being. My senior year, I would snap the tip off a vertebrae and the very next week play with a foam collar while in excruciating pain. As was always the case, those around me would remark that there was something burning inside Tim Green.

Nine

That summer before my senior year of college, I appeared to be on top of the world. At school, the dean was talking about my nomination for a Rhodes Scholarship to go with the numerous academic awards I had already garnered. Syracuse football was back to its days of winning and glory. I was being selected for every preseason All-American team that existed, and NFL scouts and agents were sniffing around me with the same hungry look that the college scouts and coaches had for me when I was a senior in high school.

The difference now was money. Oh, I was never short of cash. I had the soft summer PR job that enabled me to save enough to stay in beer and pizza through the school year. On top of that, my mom and dad were always sending a little extra cash my way, since they were way ahead of the game by not having had to pay for my college tuition. But I was looking at NFL money. I knew from seeing the rich football boosters that money—more than looks, more than awards, more than brains—was the universal lubricant. It made going through life a lot smoother. If you had money, people were going to accept you much more readily than if you didn't. If you didn't have money, people called you crazy. If you had real money, they called you eccentric. I was on the verge of real money.

Yet despite that, my nightmares raged on, strong as ever. The wintry forest was replaced by a battlefield thick with buzzing bullets and a cacophony of exploding grenades. Horrid shrieks of dying men punctuated the explosions, and the dark swirling sky was filled with surreal flying machines bent on death. As with the forest of my younger dreams, I had to cross the battlefield. To stay was unthinkable hell, to go forward was certain death. Around and around I'd go in my mind, not knowing if I wanted death and then hell or hell and then death. Those were my choices, and I would awake in a delirious fit, lying in my sweat-soaked bed until I could overcome the paralysis of fear and put myself into the shower, where only a cold pounding of water could set me free.

Worse than the nightmares of my sleep was my waking nightmare with Beth. In that summer before my final year of college, with all my merit badges and so many more obviously to come, she had cast me aside. It was Kate all over again, but how could that be?

I thought if I fought hard enough I could win her back. All I had to do was show her the logic of it: We were a perfect couple, we looked good together, we had fun together, and I was going to lay the world at her feet. It was inconceivable to me that she didn't want all that. My reasoning didn't, however, take into account the fact that Beth felt constricted by all my plotting and planning and knowing what was good for her. She resented the tightness of my grip.

That final year of school, our relationship was a series of storm fronts, wreaking havoc for a few days before giving way to relative calm, then starting up all over again. During this time, I began to hedge my bets against losing her completely. If it was going to turn out that she wasn't the one I had hoped for—the loyal woman standing beside me forever—then I didn't want to feel foolish about it later. I went out at night to prowl, using as lures my notoriety and the promise of money to come and take advantage of the bar scene, using alcohol to assuage the pain of Beth's rejection.

While I hadn't yet made the connection between my desperate need not to be rejected by my girlfriend and my rejection at birth, it was during this period, for the first time in my life, that I allowed myself to consider the mother who gave me up. I began to try to unravel some of the mysteries of my mind in the context of my adoption. It was the first time I began to consciously consider what effect being adopted had on who I was. I also began to wonder how much of who I was came from my upbringing and how much from the genetic code that was randomly paired in my mother's womb twenty-two years before. For the first time, all the incongruous things that had bothered me about myself up to that point began to make a bit of sense. If my mother was in fact a sensitive, highly emotional person and my father was a man driven, sometimes to distraction, by some internal engine to succeed, then I had nothing to be ashamed of for the way I was. I couldn't have helped it if I tried.

Then curiosity began to take root. Who was my mother and how had she come to give me up? What tragic circumstances surrounded my conception and birth? There were many romantic and wonderful possibilities. There were also nightmares so unspeakably nefarious that I had yet to imagine them.

That was how Stu, my best friend, saw the situation—as something bad waiting to happen. During a walk one night, I told him about my plan to find my biological mother.

"I don't know," he said doubtfully.

"What do you mean?" I said, surprised at his reaction.

"Everything's going good, that's all," he said. "I just don't like to see you take a chance on getting yourself hurt. Why do you need that? You've got two great parents. How do you think they're going to feel?"

"I don't know," I said. "I'm not going to tell them about it. I just want to know."

"Uh-oh," he said.

"What?"

"Don't think you can do this without them knowing," he said. "That's not going to happen. Don't kid yourself. They'll know, and I just see this thing as having a lot more downside than upside. Things are good for you right now. I just don't want to see that ruined. . . . "

Despite Stu's misgivings, I still planned on finding her, but my search didn't begin immediately. I needed time to accustom myself to the notion of having another mother out there somewhere. I also needed to consider how best to proceed. While I knew I wanted to find her, I was also content to let the idea percolate. To find her, I would need time and some of that real money. In New York, adoption records, I found out, are sealed. I would need to hire a private investigator to begin what promised to be a long arduous search.

Other things were taking my time as well. Besides my ongoing battle of wills with Beth, I was distracted by my quest for All-American honors, raising the value of my stock in the upcoming NFL draft and helping my team to win their way to a college bowl game. More pressing than any of that, though, was the situation that had evolved with my brother Kyle. During the summer Audry told me about her son, Kyle left a drug-treatment center. Unless he returned, he faced a mind-boggling two-year sentence in the state prison. He'd been sentenced to go through the drug-treatment program a year prior to that summer when he pled guilty to a petty burglary charge. Now, for some inexplicable reason, he was refusing to complete the program. The frightening jail sentence seemed imminent unless I could successfully intervene.

Some time after our return from California, Kyle had begun to experiment with drugs. It wasn't long before he was hooked on speed, grass, and LSD. The next several years were a constant battle between him and my parents. He was in and out of school, until, finally, he was placed in a disciplinary program that attempted to direct him toward a trade school, since a traditional high school education seemed out of the question. His world collapsed completely at the age of seventeen. Kyle sold a small amount of marijuana to one of his friends, and the friend refused to pay for the drugs. When Kyle went to get his money, the friend wasn't home. Unfortunately, the back door was unlocked and Kyle entered the house. He confiscated the stereo, intending to hold it as collateral until this friend gave him the money. It wasn't too many days after that when a rumpled-looking town cop pulled up next to my brother on the street and asked him to get into the patrol car. The sad-looking cop explained to Kyle that he knew he had taken the stereo. The cop told him that, in fact, the stereo belonged to the friend's mother and not the friend. The mother had worked long and hard for the $2,000 it cost her to buy it.

The avuncular cop explained that all he wanted was to know where the stereo was so he could return it to the poor woman who'd lost her most prized possession in the world. My brother, being a decent kid at heart, showed the cop where he'd hidden the stereo and was promptly arrested. My parents hired a lawyer named Leopold Nash, a hack. I don't blame my parents, neither of them had ever had any cause to hire a criminal lawyer before, and, of course, they knew next to nothing about the workings of our justice system. This kind of trouble to people like my parents was as remote as Pluto.

Nash promptly rolled over for the DA and convinced my parents and my brother that the best thing to do was plead guilty to a class-D felony. My brother would be put into the probation program where he could get the drug treatment that he needed. The treatment he really did need, but only an incompetent ass would have allowed him to plead to a class-D felony under the circumstances of his case.

Nevertheless, Kyle began rehab. The center, which was a halfway house located in a dilapidated and dangerous section of the city, was not too far from the Syracuse University campus. I would drive down and visit with Kyle almost every week. One day, he announced that he was leaving.

"What do you mean 'leaving'?" I asked. "I thought you said they told you it was going to be another month or two?"

We were sitting on the top of a half-rotten picnic table adjacent to the big ramshackle white house that held my brother and about fourteen other people in rehab. Kyle had advanced enough in the program so that he was allowed to talk with me outside in the dirt-pocked yard. With both hands, he parted the curtain of hair that normally hid his face. He looked at me with the same steel-blue eyes that still drew involuntary stares from women whenever he entered a room.

"They're worse here than I am, man."

My lips twisted in a skeptical frown. "What's that mean?"

"It means that this place is totally fucked up," he said with the simple confidence of an accountant telling you that you've had an overrun in your costs. "These people running this place are worse criminals than I ever was."

"Come on," I said, unable to hide my disgust.

"I mean it," he told me. "I was a drug addict, and I admit it. But I ain't no more. I know what my problem was and I got that beat. It doesn't make sense for me to stay here and have to get these people's permission to get out of here when they're more fucked up than me. I don't need this anymore."

I looked incredulously at him. Yes, it was easy to see that he wasn't living in a nice place. It was a garbage-strewn neighborhood with shuffling, raisin-faced bums on every corner. Half the houses had boards on their windows, and very few had escaped the kiss of spray paint. Still, it was always someone else with my brother. There was always a reason why things went awry, and the reason was never him.

"You can't just leave," I said. "They're not going to let you just leave."

"I'm leaving," he said flatly, separating himself from me by letting the hair fall back into his face. "I just thought you'd want to know."

"You can't," I stammered. "They'll put you in jail if you do. It's your probation."

He peered at me briefly through his curtain, then turned his eyes up toward the sky. An ancient leafless oak towered above us, spreading its black branches like a web of veins. Beyond was a clear field of perfect blue. I wanted him to look at me, but he wouldn't.

"I know what they'll do," he said resolutely. "I just wanted you to know. I'm not staying here. Jail is better than here. At least no one's lying about everything."

"Let them lie!" I bellowed. "Play the game, damnit! Why can't you just play the game!"

"I've got to go," he told me, shaking his head, obviously disappointed. He hopped down from the mud-colored table. "I love you, man," he said. Then he was on the porch and gone.

Kyle did leave, and the system of justice began its grind. Fifteen minutes before he was to be sentenced to the state prison, I entered the courthouse with Billy Fitzpatrick, the highest-powered defense attorney in upstate New York. Billy was the law school roommate of the man who would soon become my sports agent, if he wasn't already. Nash, a stubby man with a messy brown mop of fuzzy hair, looked about in panic. He was standing with my brother and my parents in a loose group outside the courtroom, patiently waiting to throw my brother at the mercy of a merciless court.

"What's this?" Nash said when he saw me with Fitzy.

"Tim?" my father said.

I didn't want to just jump in like that, but if my brother went to the state prison, I knew what would happen to him. I didn't know if he had a chance in life or not, but I knew he wouldn't if he ever went there.

"You're fired," I told Nash.

Nash looked from me to Fitzy and frowned. He knew there was no sense in protesting. Fitzy wouldn't be there if it wasn't for real, so without another word, he skulked out of the courthouse. My brother looked down at the floor and rubbed the dirty toe of his sneaker into a dark crack in the marble floor tile. My parents didn't know what to say. They were so distraught and confused by the actions of my brother that I would remember this day as the breaking point between them. From that point on, Kyle would come to rely on me almost exclusively.

"Okay," Fitzy said with an authoritative nod, "I'll be back."

Ten minutes after disappearing down the side hall, Fitzy returned from the judge's chambers.

"You're facing two years in the state prison for walking out of the treatment center and breaking the conditions of your parole," he told my brother sternly. "That's the sentence for a class-D felony. Now I got him to do this, either you go back today or you'll do three months in the county jail."

My brother looked up and said, "I'll do three months. I'm not going back."

Fitzy shrugged. "Okay, it's a good deal."

Just before the snowy winter set in, the All-American teams started naming their players. AP, Kodak, Walter Kamp, UPI, *Sporting News.* Each of them included me. Our team was selected to go to the first bowl game of many that marked the resurgence of Syracuse football to a national power. It was the height of my popularity in the community. I couldn't go to a restaurant, a bar, or a grocery store without being pointed at or asked for an autograph. My money was no good. Dinner and drinks were always free.

That meant everyone at the jail recognized me as well. Every Sunday I would go to the grocery store and put together a couple of bags of junk food for my brother. The county jail sat on a high hill outside the city. Alone, I'd drive the winding roads past the dreary yawning gravel pits that lined the way. Half my time at the jail was spent signing autographs for guards and prisoners, the other half was spent talking to my brother across a linoleum table in the big white-walled visitor's room.

Our team returned from the bowl game a few days before Christmas. With my college eligibility now spent, my agent came out of the closet and cut me a deal with a local car dealer. A day later, I got the brand-new truck I'd always wanted. On Sunday, I put the key to my old car in a jewelry box and tied it up in a clumsy white ribbon. My brother was getting out in just a few weeks, and I wanted him to have some wheels so he could flee to wherever it was he wanted to restart his life. I had no idea then if that were possible. It seemed that over the past several years, Kyle had done nothing but deceive everyone, including himself.

It wasn't until later that spring that I read in the newspaper about how they were closing down the halfway house my brother had walked out of. It seems one of the counselors was murdered by two coworkers in a dispute over the control of a drug ring that was being operated out of the house. Kyle, it turned out, was right all along.

Between football and school and Kyle, it didn't seem like I had any time to think. But it was during those long drives to the jail that I really thought most about my mother. Besides being rare solitary moments in a hectic life, I was confronted during those drives with the obvious differences between me and my brother. He was adopted. I was adopted. We grew up in the same house, with the same parents, under the same set of rules. I was getting ready to sign a million-dollar sports contract and was graduating at the top of my class. He was waiting to get out of jail, hoping he'd kicked his drug habit. I mean that in no way disparagingly toward Kyle; I loved him then and love him still. We had, however, become two drastically different people. The question was why?

Ten

Of course, the reason for the many differences between my brother and me was simple, and it finally goaded me into action. I was different from my brother, my parents, my sister, everyone I knew, because I was part of someone entirely different, someone I didn't know. I began to use what clout I had in the community in an attempt to find my biological mother. I had covert meetings with politicians, lawyers, and influential businessmen, seeking any help someone might be able to give me in getting my hands on my adoption records.

I confess that I felt ashamed during these meetings, coming hat in hand to men of power in order to beg for their help. We would meet for lunch or in dark-paneled offices where shapely secretaries would bring us coffee in quiet servitude. And every time I explained the situation, I would sit there in my ill-fitting suit and tie and feel as though I'd been stripped completely naked in front of these men. It wasn't that a single one of them disparaged me. It was that to get their help, I had to confess what had happened to me, that I had been given up, discarded. All my honors and awards, all my prestige seemed to fall to my feet in a rumpled pile. I couldn't shake the feeling that I was a disappointment to them.

It was the thought of those records that kept me going. I knew that they must lay in a random file buried in some government office. I could see that file in my mind. I often imagined it sitting there stuffed between other manila containers holding other people's histories as surely as a vault, of no use to anyone but me, holding the keys to who I was.

No one would help. It became obvious fairly quickly that while the men of power were more than happy to meet with me and talk about the upcoming NFL draft or the state of next year's SU football team, no one was going to go out on a limb to try and help me do what appeared to be nearly impossible. Records like mine were legally sacrosanct and could only be obtained by someone with deep-level state access. To help me, that same someone would have to be willing to commit a criminal act. The obvious upside would be nothing more than helping me to satisfy what people perceived as a mere curiosity on my part. It wasn't going to happen, and I couldn't blame a soul. I did, however, discover one legal possibility.

I was affronted by these laws. How could the faceless state keep me from finding the woman who gave me life? On an emotional level, it was infuriating. On an intellectual level, I approached it in much the same way as I had the rest of life: a puzzle to be solved, a badge to be won. Like every other prospective NFL player who has a problem, I called my agent.

John Marchiano had already proven himself to be well connected in the Syracuse area when he helped me get Billy Fitzpatrick to handle Kyle's sentencing. When I went to him with this problem, John secured for me a private detective named Dale Doyle from the nearby town of Utica. While I was excited about Doyle and the possibilities a detective entailed, I was also disconcerted. There were two forces at work inside me: one pushing me forward in my search, the other holding me back. I'm certain now that in one sense I was quite afraid of finding my mother. It was like waiting for the outcome of some serious medical tests: desperate to know, but locked up by the terror of discovering something bad.

John had Doyle do some preliminary research, then connected us via conference call. Doyle laid out the ground rules for me. The state of New York had something called an adoption registry. It was the best hope for an adopted person trying to find his biological mother. If the child registered and the mother had also filed with the registry, the state would put the two parties into contact. Both mother and child, however, must have registered independently of each other. The state would make no contact otherwise. There was some bad news that went along with this as well.

"You need your parents' signatures," Doyle told me.

"My parents?"

"Yes."

"My parents don't have anything to do with this," I said. "That doesn't make sense."

"They do," Doyle explained. "When they adopted you, they were guaranteed that all the records would be sealed. It's part of the deal in this state. When people adopt a child, they don't want the biological parents suddenly showing up and messing up their lives. That's why you have to get their signature to register."

"I don't want my parents in this," I said, sickened. "I don't want them to know."

There I was, on the precipice of a big contract and an NFL career. How could I let my parents, the people who had helped me get there, think that somehow I felt they hadn't been enough? It wasn't true, but that's what they might think: that all the washed clothes, the hugs, the caring for me when I was sick, meant nothing to me. I just couldn't do that to them.

Doyle hesitated on the phone.

"Well, there is some information you can get without anyone's permission," he said. "It's not much, but it might help. We can take a look at it anyway."

The state, it turned out, would give me what was called nonidentifying information without anyone else's consent or signature. The "nonidentifying" information would tell me something about my mother and possibly my father without disclosing any names of people or places that could lead to their discovery.

"It's pretty vague stuff," Doyle said. "But you never know. There might be some information in there that we could use and possibly track her down. At least, we could start there and then move to the registry later on if we hit a wall. It's not going to be the cheapest way to go. . . . "

"I don't care," I said. "Let's try it."

Letting my parents know of my search was out of the question. It was an unthinkable act.

Doyle sent me to the Bureau of Vital Statistics. The office was located in the basement of the civic center in downtown Syracuse. I was relieved that the owlish man behind the desk seemed to know nothing of football or anyone who played it. He didn't look at me with any more interest than he did at the large round clock on the wall that still held three hours of time before the workday ended. It was a simple form, actually. I filled it in and gave my agent's address as the place to send the information. I knew from Doyle that it would be months before the bureaucratic machinery of New York State turned enough cogs to spit out the information I sought. All I could do now was wait and dream about the people who were responsible for my existence.

As an English major at Syracuse, my education included the study of several stories where lost children were later found. After reading books like *Tom Jones*, *Oliver Twist*, and *David Copperfield*, it wasn't hard for me to imagine my own history, full of noble and romantic characters, where some cruel twist of fate had kept me from the couple that was responsible for my existence. I don't think this was a healthy thing. Certainly, it was dangerous. But there was no way I could have known then what I know now: Most stories of adoption are filled with tragedy and sadness, most children given up are inconvenient bumps in the road, and it is a rare day indeed when a son finds his mother and the story has a happy ending. Since I had no idea of these things, I dreamed on and played out one of the most exciting events of my life, the NFL draft, having no idea that within a month's time I would meet the woman who would change my life.

Eleven

Despite my farewell to Audry almost a year before college graduation, Beth and I continued to separate and rejoin the way people will when they are in a terminal relationship that they just can't let pass away. When the day of the NFL draft finally arrived, we were still trying to make it work. Beth was with me in my parents' living room on that glorious day when the Atlanta Falcons chose me in the first round. She was there when the local media burst through my parents' family room door like a geyser, anxious to get everyone's immediate reaction. And she was right beside me in the AP wire picture that went out across the country, a young man and his young love striking it rich: the American Dream. Then she was gone the next day without so much as a blink, back to Cornell to take her exams and wrap up her undergraduate degree, among other things.

For my own part, I was enjoying my final days of college by participating in an endless cycle of strenuous workouts during the day and endless bouts of drinking during the night. As incongruous as the two may seem, it was actually perfect training for my life as an NFL player, where alcohol seems to be an integral part of the strenuous physical regimen.

I was enlightened as to Beth's extracurricular activities one morning during that time when I was on my way to lunch, which was really breakfast, with my ex-roommate Todd Norley. Todd had been our team's quarterback, and we'd lived together until our senior year, when he'd gotten married. We were still close, though, and got together as often as our disparate lives would allow.

Before he was married, Todd and I were inseparable. We lived our college days to their fullest. We had the kind of relationship that made other guys jealous. Although together constantly, we never seemed to rub one another the wrong way. We were also as honest to each other as we were to ourselves. So when he told me what he'd heard, I didn't question its veracity.

The sun was shining that day. There was a warm wind blowing fat cumulus clouds across an otherwise clear blue sky. The leaves on the trees had the color and smell of fresh limes. We drove with the windows of my truck wide open. My hat was pulled tight and low on my forehead to keep the sun out of my eyes and the hangover contained to the upper reaches of my skull. Todd, a happy victim of married life, was feeling quite fine, at least physically. Something else seemed to be eating away at him.

"What's up?" I mumbled, wincing in pain just from the effort of speaking.

"I don't want to tell you," he said solemnly, "but I have to. . . . "

Whatever animal had taken up residence in my gut since the night before rolled over and began to twitch, as if overtaken by some kind of epileptic fit. I never took bad news well.

"What?" I said, fighting panic.

"I didn't know if I should say anything," he labored, "but I figured if it was me, I'd want to know. I'd want you to tell me. . . . "

"What the hell *is* it?" I demanded.

My friend looked at me sadly and said, "I was on campus yesterday and you know that girl Clara that you know?"

I did a quick short-term memory search: Clara, a six-foot blond temptress, baleful eyes, a body that wouldn't quit.

"Yeah, what about *her*?"

"She's from Ithaca, you know. . . . "

"So?"

"Well, shit . . . she asked me what was going on with you and Beth. I guess she was home over the weekend and she met this guy in some bar. Somehow, it came up that she was going to Syracuse and the guy asked her if she knew you."

"Me?"

"Yeah, the guy told her that . . . the guy told her that he was living with the girl who used to be your girlfriend, Beth."

I had pulled my truck over to the side of the road. *Used to be?* Now I looked at him in disbelief.

"You sure?" I said.

"Yeah," he told me, obviously sorry, "I'm sure. I asked her three times about it. I didn't want to get it wrong. I thought I should tell you."

"You should have," I told him. "I'm glad you did."

I whipped around and dropped Todd off back at his apartment, then raced back to my own place. Breakfast could wait until dinner. I pulled across the lawn right up to the front door and hopped out of my truck without bothering to close the door. I plucked the phone from the counter and nearly pulled the wires out of the wall. I was already dialing when I heard the screen door ratchet back and slam shut behind me.

"Hello?"

She sounded half-asleep, as if she'd just taken a bath, gotten laid, and smoked a joint. Something was wrong. Everything was wrong. I could sense him there, right there beside her! I didn't hear anything, not even breathing. She didn't say anything, but I could sense him, rolling over and languidly tossing a hairy leg over her smooth bare hip.

"You bitch," I hissed. "How could you screw some guy in the bed that I bought for you with my own *money*?!"

I slammed the phone down and pieces of it burst across the room in three different directions.

"To me? She did this to *me*?" I bellowed. I raged and stamped and slammed my fists against anything that wouldn't break bones. "To *me? To me? She did this to me?*"

It was unthinkable. I thought I had accomplished enough to hedge against this sort of abandonment. But in the end, all the honors and awards and accomplishments I had to my name weren't enough. I treated my girlfriend like a queen, proclaiming to the world that I belonged to her, lavishing her with all the passion I could muster. Even money was forthcoming. I foolishly thought that's what bonded a woman to a man. Respect, loud proclamations of love, passion, and money—weren't they the cement of acceptance? I had given this woman everything I had to give and still it wasn't enough. I didn't know then that trophies and accomplishments aren't the currency with which love and loyalty are purchased.

When I purged myself of as much poison as was possible at that moment, I did the only thing I could do: I went on a rampage. It wasn't that I hadn't been unfaithful to Beth before. I had. What, with the tumultuous uncertainties of our relationship? I was known to wake up in a strange dorm room from time to time or run down a pretty girl at last call the night after a big game. I'll be honest: It wasn't that I hadn't done it before, it was that when I had done it, it had been in response to some spurning from the girl who was supposed to love me. When she would pass on coming up for a weekend, dishing out some lame excuse to be with her friends, or go on spring break without me, those were the times when I'd slip. But living with someone? Flat-out shacking up? I lost my mind.

My reputation, sullied already in the minds of many coeds, went from dubious to infamous. I was relentless in my pursuit of one-night conquests, intent on proving to myself, if not Beth, that women did want me. I was a package deal, and a bargain. I behaved in a way that shames me to this day. I played on my name. I played on my status as a star football player. I played on the fact that everyone expected me to soon be rich. It worked like a charm.

It was during the initial stages of my rampage that I met the woman whom I said would change my life. It wasn't my mother. It was my wife. I was leaving my apartment one day on my way to a karate workout with Dougy Marone, a 310-pound buddy of mine who had been drafted by the Raiders. We were just about to get into my truck when a red Audi Coupe pulled up next to us. A girl got out. She was without makeup, wore a baggy, gray cotton sweat suit, and her hair was pinned to her head by an old bandanna. Dougy introduced us. He was giddy, not a pretty sight for a guy that big.

I shook hands with her, said hello and good-bye, and got into the truck. Her name was Illyssa, a nice name.

"What was that all about?" I said, disgusted with his syrupy fawning.

"Aw, man," he told me in his thick Bronx accent, "don't even think about it."

"Think about what?" I said, incredulously.

"I know you," he said. "I know you. But don't do it. You'll make a fool out of yourself. Don't even think about thinking about it."

I kept looking at him as I fired up the truck.

"You're crazy," I muttered, throwing the vehicle into gear. "I mean she was nice, but what's the big deal?"

He looked at me slyly and said, "Aw no, you're not getting me like that. I know you. Don't even think about it, I'm telling you. You'll really make a fool out of yourself. She's got a boyfriend, and she won't go for it. Don't even try. That's all I'm telling you."

We went to the dojo and punched foam targets for a few hours. We lifted weights until we were dizzy and finished off by running until Dougy threw up. Then we were ready. After a light dinner, we started in on another night of heavy drinking.

I had dropped the subject of Illyssa since the truck ride, and so had Dougy, although he looked at me sideways every so often throughout the day and shook his head. As far as I was concerned, the poor oaf was already acting like one of those crazy L.A. Raiders he was soon to become. I wasn't thinking about the parking lot incident at all by the time we walked through the door of a place called Braggs. We cut the huge line, waved and nodded to the bouncers, greeted the bartenders with smiles, and immediately started slugging down free long-neck beers. When I saw her, I knew exactly what he had been talking about, exactly why he had presumed I would do everything in my power to be near her.

Gone were the baggy sweats, the ratty bandanna, and the sleep-swollen eyes. There she was in a pair of jeans, a crisp, clean white blouse, a dark blazer, and blood-red cowboy boots, surrounded by an aurora of dark radiant hair. Her bottle-green eyes sat an intelligent distance on either side of her streamlined nose. Her lips were unpainted, yet full and red and adorned by a slight but pleasant smile. It was as if I were seeing her for the first time. The lights and the students and the noise of the place all seemed to orbit her as if she were the sun itself. I felt that same pull. It wasn't beauty alone that drew me to her. Her face spoke of kindness and confidence.

"How do you say her name again?" I said to my friend, pointing her out.

"Illyssa," he told me, rhyming the middle part with "miss." "Where you going?"

"I see what you meant, and I don't care," I told him, already locking eyes with her as I crossed the loud crowded space of that college bar.

We talked, and after I'd had enough to drink, I even danced, not because I had ever taken a shine to dancing but just as an excuse to be close to Illyssa and look at her without having her friends hovering over her shoulder. After all, it was just a couple of dances. But when the music got so damn convoluted that I had to hopelessly abandon the floor, I still stayed close to her and stared into her eyes.

Her friends circled us like vultures, and I could tell they were all impatiently waiting for her to reduce me to a spent carcass just for having the audacity to continue to stare and drink and stare and drink and talk and laugh and flat-out refuse to let her get away. But the more I shooed those vultures away with my evil eye, the more indignant and impatient they became and the closer they swooped.

Finally, I said, "Let's get out of here."

"Where?" she replied candidly.

Her eyes told me the whole story. Her eyes told me she liked me, but they warned me, too. They warned me not to make a mistake, not to act too rashly. Those eyes saw right through me and everything I was about. I liked that about her. I wanted her to see everything. I wanted her to know the worst as well as the best.

"How about someplace to eat," I suggested as a novelty. "I'm starving. Are you hungry?"

"No, but I'll go someplace with you. Let me tell my friends."

She moved among her friends, who were legion, and they in turn cast brazenly hateful stares my way. I, after all, was a bad man. When she returned, she had some guy in tow.

"This is Bruce," she told me. "He's a friend of mine. He's going to come with us."

I eyed Bruce up and down. But I knew the conditions were not negotiable. On our way from the bar to the diner, I did my best to shake him—subtle hints, malignant stares, friendly pats on the back—but to his credit, he knew his mission and he stuck to her like a faithful retriever. Finally, I stopped trying and just ordered some food and pretended he wasn't there. After a while, that worked, and I was pouring my heart out to this girl I hadn't known for more than twelve hours.

The night ended too quickly. Bruce hustled her from the diner as if her carriage were about to turn into a pumpkin. After they were gone, I sat there alone for a while and stewed. I didn't trust what my heart was telling me. How, after all, could I have met the perfect woman in a parking lot, not recognize her for what she was, then have a sudden epiphany in a college bar that would change my life forever? Maybe I was being influenced too much by the books I had read. Maybe it was my desperate need, in light of my troubles with Beth, to have some good and beautiful woman to loyally attach herself to me, thereby proving to myself that I was worthy. Whatever the cause of my distraction, my mind wrestled my heart to the floor and urged me to carry on as if nothing out of the ordinary had happened. It was my weak and foolish heart, after all, that had caused me so much pain of late. My body, too, ached for something warm, something to fill the cool and lonely space beside me through the night. I took one last bite of something Illyssa had left on her plate and made my way back into the murky nocturnal habitat of college coeds in search of easier prey.

Twelve

During those next few weeks, mysterious forces repeatedly threw us together. The day after we met, I walked into a campus restaurant, uncharacteristically alone, and there she was. I joined her and her evil friends, and we had a good talk. I happened upon her two out of the next four nights. Then we purposely started to meet. We liked each other. As incongruous as it seemed—her being a devoted girlfriend, me being a notorious rake—we had a lot in common. Despite my behavior at the time, what I wanted most was to marry a nice, smart, morally upright girl like Illyssa who wanted more than anything to be a wife and a mother. She apparently wanted someone like me if or when they were ready to behave themselves.

One night we were out, and I told Illyssa about my ex-girlfriend, about how I always seemed to want to be around her more than she wanted to be around me. She told me she was the same way with her boyfriend, a guy she was having serious doubts about. Without saying so directly, we let it be known that we each thought the other had been casting pearls to swine. I tried to lean over and kiss her, but she gently held me at bay and averted her lips. I was captivated by her loyalty. Despite the ill feelings she had toward her boyfriend, even the expectation that she would soon be rid of him, she still wouldn't have anything to do with me that went beyond a good conversation. I respected that. It was how I wished my ex-girlfriend had been: true-blue. Not that I had deserved it.

Is it possible in today's world to have a love affair without even a kiss? If not, then I don't know what it was that happened to us during those last few weeks of school. I explain it like this: We became good friends, but it was more. One night I climbed into her apartment through a second-story window. I was drunk, and I smelled of another woman's perfume. I explained as best I could that there was a girl sleeping at my place whom I couldn't wake up and couldn't bear to wake up next to in the morning. I know, I was repulsive. I think I went to her the way you might go to confession and spill out the worst of your deeds to a forgiving priest. Looking back, I think I wanted Illyssa to see the worst in me, the lecherous drunk. I don't think I wanted to take another chance with my heart, following the treacherous path to rejection. Even the best of me hadn't been enough for the two girlfriends I'd loved before. I wasn't going to let myself love another until I was certain she would love me back. I had no idea back then that Illyssa could see through ruses laid by people more clever than I. I only knew that despite my condition she let me stay, sternly warning me to keep my hands to myself.

I staggered into her bathroom and inquired which toothbrush was hers. She showed me without a hint of horror, although later, without telling me, she would throw it away. I slopped on some paste and began to pull off my clothes as I brushed away. She smiled in disbelief.

"What are you doing?"

"Taking off my clothes," I muttered absently through the paste.

By now, I was down to my boxers, and I spit out the paste and rinsed my mouth.

"It's no big deal," I told her, swaying from all that I had to drink. "It's like shorts."

"You're not sleeping in my bed like that!" she told me.

It was too late. I was already between her sheets, lying on my back with my eyes closed, spinning out of control in my alcoholic haze.

"It's no big deal," I murmured. The bedclothes were soft and smelled so clean I felt like I was in a hotel. The cotton comforter was dark like the night and speckled with yellow points like evening stars. Everything was soft and safe and peaceful, and I was quickly falling asleep. With a sigh and a look to the ceiling, Illyssa slid into the bed beside me in a pair of silk pajamas. A wonderful smile spread through me as I reached out and touched her long soft hair. With her head nestled into the crook of my arm, she laid her hand across my chest.

"You're skin is so soft," she whispered.

I felt so good. It was one of those moments where I would have been happy to die. Instead, I slept, and so did she.

Within a matter of days, the semester came to a close and Illyssa and I had yet to kiss. I was packing my things into an eclectic assortment of boxes with my apartment doors wide open and my truck half full when she appeared at my bedroom door.

"I came to say good-bye," she said. She looked genuinely sad.

"Hey," I told her brandishing my last pair of socks, "I'm almost done. It's an awesome day. I'm going to the lake to get some sun. Come with me. We'll talk."

"I can't," she said.

"I'll get a six-pack of beer," I promised.

"I imagine you will," she said, a small smile breaking the sadness on her face. She didn't drink.

"Really, come with me."

"You know . . . I would," she said, "but my boyfriend is coming to help me move my stuff back home and I can't do that to him."

"You're boyfriend is a schmuck," I reminded her. "Just tell him you got hung up with something. Let him wait. This is the guy that's not even so nice to you."

"I know," she said, looking up at me with her big dark-green eyes, "but he's my boyfriend. I just wanted to tell you thanks. I had a great time with you these past few weeks. I feel like we're really friends."

"We are."

"I know. I don't know," she said, looking at the empty walls and the bent barren nails I was leaving behind, "I hope we meet up again sometime. . . . "

"Do you really mean all that stuff you said about how you just want to get married and have kids and stuff?"

"Yes," she said, blushing, "when I find the right person. That's what I want."

"And all that stuff about cooking? You meant that, huh? I mean, it's just because I think that stuff is great. . . . "

She smiled at me big and shook her head, not knowing if I was for real.

"Here," she said, handing me a card. "I got you a graduation card. I wrote my number in it in case you ever . . . I don't know, if you ever get down to the city."

"Hey," I said, taking the card and taking the liberty to give her a hug. "Thanks. Come with me. I don't want to say good-bye."

"I have to go," she whispered. Then she left.

I watched her wave as she slid behind the wheel of that red coupe. I figured it was the last time I would ever see her, and it was my turn to look sad. I figured she was just the kind of girl I needed. But like they say, timing is everything. I was off to Atlanta and she had a boyfriend. Her loyalty, the very thing that made me adore her, was the same damn thing that didn't even give us a chance.

I had a couple of weeks between graduation and then I had to be down in Atlanta to start summer training. The coaches wanted me there to learn the defensive schemes so I would be ready to play right away. When you're a first-round pick and they put all that money into you, they want you out on the field. In the meantime, I moved my base of operations temporarily back into my parent's house. It was kind of rough on them, having me wheel into the house at three A.M., if at all, but they were great sports. I think they were happy to see me without Beth. To them, she had been a millstone around my neck. They appreciated the things I had accomplished. They were proud of me to a fault. It was nice to be home.

It was during this brief stay at home, on a day when I awoke with a mild hangover at about eleven in the morning, that I got the notion into my head to check through my parents' papers. The idea came on me as unexpectedly as when you catch the flu. I don't know where it came from. I hadn't heard from Doyle or the state, and I had been so busy with graduation, Illyssa, and my bad behavior that I hadn't given my search all that much thought. I figured there couldn't be too much in my parents' documents that could tell me about my adoption, but one never knew. The house was empty. They were both at work. A little surreptitious reconnaissance, I thought, beat the hell out of asking them, as Doyle suggested, straight out for any information they had regarding my biological mother.

My mom kept a house about as neat as anyone I've ever run across. This made it pretty easy to locate their important papers. There were only a few places in the entire house where everything wasn't easily identifiable just by opening a closet or pulling a drawer. There was, I knew, a box in my parents' bedroom closet that had no markings and no apparent purpose. Of course, it was that box that contained exactly the papers I wanted to peruse, and I found more than I had expected.

There was an old article written in a company newspaper published by the General Electric plant where my father had worked at the time of my adoption. Apparently, I was the first in the program that was set up through the company to aid its workers who were seeking to adopt children. There were photos of me as a very young boy in the company of my parents, both of whom wore the kind of cat glasses that were in style in the early sixties. I scanned the article thoroughly, seeking any bit of information that might help me. The entire article yielded only the name of the adoption agency. There was nothing I could use. Still, there were other papers, so I pressed on.

Within a minute, I found a single sheet that listed what I knew must be my medical records at the time of birth. It gave me things like my height and weight, but went so far as to describe the type of delivery: a six-hour labor under general anesthesia where LOA forceps were used to deliver me. In a strange and remote way, this information made me feel connected to my mother for the first time. It was the first bit of news that I had regarding her in any way. It was minute, but it was something. I now knew the circumstances under which she had delivered me. It somehow gave me joy to know even the smallest detail, as if it made her real. I removed this paper and took it to the drugstore, where I copied it immediately before replacing it in my parents' things. I said a word to no one. I had no idea then that it would be the linchpin of my search.

The day soon came when I had to pack my bags and get ready to start a new life in a new city in a new state, and that scared the hell out of me. I waited until my parents were clear of the house before I called Beth. There was no sense in getting them upset about what a sap I was. Beth and I hadn't spoken since I'd broken the phone. She actually seemed glad to hear from me. She still had feelings. I had feelings.

"Listen," I told her, desperate not to be alone, "I'm leaving for Atlanta tomorrow on a one o'clock flight. Come with me."

She took a quick breath, and I knew I'd caught her off guard.

"Look," I said, "you've done some things, I've done some things. Let's just forget it all. We've been together for three years. We love each other. Let's just put everything bad behind us and start our life over the way it should have been all along. Let's just forget about all the crap."

"I want to go with you," she told me, "I just don't think right now is good. I think I want to spend the summer here and just figure out what I want to do with my life. . . . "

"Can't you figure it out in Atlanta?" I said. I could feel myself starting to boil. "We can have it all," I told her, "but you've got to come with me. From the beginning, I want you there. You could leave now and get back tonight or early in the morning, I don't care. Just be on that plane with me, Beth, and we'll start over. I promise I'll never bring up everything that's happened. Come with me."

"I want to," she said, but her voice faltered. "But can't you just give me some time to think?"

"No," I said. Enough was enough. She'd been thinking on and off for three years whether she wanted me or not, and I was offering her a onetime deal. "I want you to come with me tomorrow on that plane. If you're not, that's it. I mean it. You're either with me or you're not."

That night, I went over to Stu's house.

"I've got a good one for you," Stu told me at the door.

We watched the old black-and-white Lawrence Olivier film *Rebecca*. It was the perfect tonic for me: the story of a good man ruined by a bad woman. I'm not saying that was my situation verbatim, but it felt good to pretend I was Olivier, mortally wronged by Beth. It was either that or admit what I suspected deep down: I had a fissure-like flaw that was somehow only obvious to women who knew me well, including the mother who gave me away. At the end of the movie, Olivier was resuscitated by Joan Fontaine, suggesting hope for all mankind, even me. Colleen went to bed. Stu and I put on denim jackets to prowl the neighborhood. The sky was clear, and Stu pointed out the Pleiades, Atlas's seven daughters who were metamorphosed into stars.

I had already told Stu about my ultimatum to Beth.

"She's not going to come," I said.

"Beth?"

"Yeah."

Stu shook his head, doubting it, too.

"But you never know," he reminded me.

We walked in silence for a few moments, our eyes on the stars, until I said, "I met a good woman."

"They're out there," my friend told me.

"You've got one," I said. "That's what I want, a woman who'll be there, like Joan Fontaine . . . like Colleen."

"She is good."

I told him then about Illyssa.

"I think she's like that, too," I concluded, "but I'll probably never see her again."

"Why not?" Stu said.

I shrugged. "She's got her life. I'm going to Atlanta. . . . "

There was no need to tell him that I'd proven myself to her to be a drunken whoremonger.

"Well, you never know," he said.

"No, you never do."

I woke late the next day and didn't get into the shower until a little after ten. I got out, dried off, got dressed amid the jungle of boxes in my room, and went downstairs. The light on the answering machine was blinking, and I hit the play button. It was Beth.

"Tim, I love you baby, and I want us to be together. We have to be together . . . I'm still at school, but I need to talk to you. Don't go without calling me. I've got an idea, and I know it can work. Call me. I love you. Bye."

I looked at my watch. It was 10:30. The only way she could make that plane was if she had a Formula One and there was an Autobahn between Syracuse and Cornell. I erased the message and finished packing my bags. The phone seemed to hover near me like a small but vicious pet waiting to attack. I shouldered an oversized duffel bag bulging with clothes and looked at that damn thing one more time before shaking my head resolutely and walking out the door. Atlanta was waiting. I was alone, again.

Thirteen

The Falcons put me up in a roadside motel called the Falcon Inn, right off Route 85, about thirty miles north of the city. The motel was directly adjacent to the team's practice facility and offices. Between the two buildings lay three football fields, like a lush green oasis in the midst of the baked-brown Georgia heat. The idea was for me to meet with my position coach, Gill Harper, in the mornings and lift weights and run with the rest of the team in the afternoon.

Every day except Saturday and Sunday, Gill and I would go through the playbook, learning new defensive terminology and working on specific physical drills that would enable me to be ready to play as soon as my contract was hammered out. Like every NFL team, the Falcons wanted me, as their number-one draft choice, to be ready to take the field with the starting unit in the fall and make spectacular plays right away. That's what they were going to pay me the big money for. Meanwhile, at the Falcon Inn, I was the only player. The rest of the guys I worked out with in the afternoon were all veterans, busy with their own lives in the middle of the off-season. They had families, social lives, and businesses that took them away just as soon as they were done working out. I was just a raw rookie who was going to make a lot of money and probably take a job away from someone who was already everyone's friend.

Gill and the lifting kept me busy, but not busy enough for a kid with a punctured heart. Despite my ultimatum and knowing for some time that Beth and I probably would never work, actually being down there alone was harder than I'd imagined. Every minute I was alone in my room was painful. I felt so sorry for myself that I would actually throw myself down on the bed and sob. In that way, I suppose I hadn't changed. I pined for Beth and most especially for the good times she and I had had. Try as I might to invoke some animosity, comparing her in my mind to Lawrence Olivier's faithless Rebecca, only the good things about the last three years with her would come to mind. I was completely distraught at being in Atlanta all alone without a single friend. After the first two days and the loneliest nights I can ever remember, I called my mom back home.

"How is it?" she asked.

"Fine, Mom," I lied. "I'm working hard."

I told her as much as I could about my teammates and my coaches and what little of Atlanta I had seen.

"Hey, Mom," I finally said, "in my bedroom there's a box of notebooks. It's not sealed up or anything. Would you mind looking in there for me and looking for a graduation card I got from that girl Illyssa. I think I told you about her."

"The girl that likes to cook?" my mom asked, in no way disguising her delight.

"Yeah, that's her. Will you see if you can find that card, Mom? She wrote her telephone number in there, and I wanted to just give her a call and see how she's doing."

"Hang on."

I waited for a while, breathing deep the mildewed funk that had overrun the efforts of a flagging air conditioner. Then the phone rattled.

"Got it!" my mom said triumphantly.

"Great, Mom, thanks."

As soon as we hung up, I dialed Illyssa's number. It was about four in the afternoon. I was faced with the prospect of eating alone in the hotel restaurant with a sparse crowd of truckers and salesmen working for companies too cheap to put them up in a real place. After that, I'd call everyone I knew. That routine, I knew, would never get me through the entire month I was supposed to be there working out. I was desperate for reinforcements. Illyssa happened to be home.

"I can't believe you're calling," she said, sounding genuinely pleased.

"I know," I said, "but, well, you said to give you a call sometime, so . . ."

"Well, how are things going?" she wanted to know.

I told her the truth. I was more miserable than I could remember. I told her about Beth. I told her how I had envisioned the excitement of going to a new city and taking it by storm, having fun with a bunch of guys, going out every night, working hard during the day, starting everything all over.

"I'm about a million miles from nowhere," I said. "I'm lonely as all hell and I don't know a single person. . . .

"So," I continued, "I got this crazy idea. I know it's kind of nuts, but I was thinking that I'd really love to have you come down here for a few days and visit me. I mean, I'd get you your own hotel room and all that, you know, I'm not trying to pull anything on you. But I just thought, well, if you were here, we could kind of hang out together, go to dinner, check out the area, rent some movies at night or something, just hang out like we did."

The silence emptied into my stomach like a ladle of molten lead. Then she half chuckled and said, "You're not going to believe this. . . . I just came from the beach. I just told my boyfriend that it was over between us. I really meant it. I guess I finally got fed up. . . . I think I could come."

"Great! How about tomorrow morning?"

"Tomorrow?"

"Why not?"

"I don't know," she said. "I guess I could. Why not? Okay."

The next day, I picked her up at the airport after practice. The head coach had magnanimously loaned me a dealer car that he'd been given as a perk. Illyssa's plane was early, and she was waiting for me on the curb. I loaded her bag into the trunk, gallantly opened her door, and drove off with a map and the address of what was supposed to be a very good Italian restaurant.

She told me she could only stay for a day, but I was thankful for even that. We had a fine meal and then went to the theater to see *A*

Room with a View. The movie was based on the E. M. Forster novel, set in Victorian England, my favorite period of literature. It was the perfect show to see, romantic and nice, passionate but dignified. When we got back to the hotel, I carried Illyssa's bag into her room and turned toward her.

"I want to kiss you," I said softly.

"All right," she whispered, smiling nervously. After all, we'd spent the night together in the same bed but had never kissed. The fact that we'd been so close without intimacy made the moment almost embarrassing.

I closed the space between us and put my arms around her waist. She tilted her head up and met my lips with her eyes wide open. Her lips, pretty and full, were soft, and her kiss was as gentle as her voice.

"That was nice," she said.

We kissed again, more passionately this time.

"I want you," I told her in a gravelly voice.

"You can't," she said. "You don't know what you want. I don't know what I want either. I won't do that until we both know."

Still, I couldn't help myself from trying, from searching and imploring her. I was glad when I realized that she meant exactly what she'd said. So many of us don't. We spent the night together regardless, with the invisible boundary between us ending just the other side of a kiss.

The next morning, her one day turned into two. She called the airline and moved her reservation back a day. The next day, she did the same. On the fourth day, after I finished working out, we went to a sandy beach at the park on Lake Lanier. We spread our towels and lay back in the sun. I drank two cold bottles of beer and fell asleep. When I awoke, my upper lip was damp from sweat and Illyssa was leaning over me, staring down from in front of the sun. Her hair wafted in the gentle breeze and tickled my face.

"I had a dream," I told her. "I dreamed we were married. We lived in a house, and over the fireplace there was a big portrait of us and our kids. It was nice. . . . "

"It sounds nice," she said gently.

"I'd like that someday," I said lazily with a yawn. "To have kids, a wife, all that. I'm not saying . . . "

"No," she said, "I know. I want that, too . . . one day. When it's right."

Four days turned into five. Finally, ten days later, she really did have to go. Our romance reminded me of one of Stu's black-and-white movies: warm, even passionate, without being sexual. I kept my distance except for our occasional kisses. We explored the parks and restaurants and shops in Atlanta and the surrounding area. Every night, we'd rent a movie and most times fall asleep, fully clothed, on top of one of the beds in her room. During those ten glorious days and nights, the sting of loneliness was assuaged, and I fell in love in a way I never had before. It was love born from respect as well as adoration.

She was nice to everyone who crossed her path. Although she'd grown up in a world of limousines and servants, Illyssa treated the women who cleaned the hotel or the guy who pumped the gas into the car with the same dignity she afforded the owner of the team when she met him at a barbecue. It was fascinating to me to see a woman who came from the upper class act as if there were no such thing. Everyone to her was a person. She seemed as impervious to the grease under one person's fingernails as to the diamonds around the neck of another.

At the same time, she was no pushover. Far from that. While she'd sit demurely at a restaurant, effortlessly using the most proper manners, if someone crossed Illyssa, they knew about it. At an expensive French restaurant one night, the maître d', who had a marvelous accent, told us we'd have to wait quite a while. He also got huffy with me because I had a shirt with no collar under my jacket. I was red-faced and ready to walk out with my tail between my legs when Illyssa stopped me with a firm grip on my arm.

"You're not an owner are you?" she said pleasantly to the snooty maître d'.

"Pardon *me*, mademoiselle?" he said, obviously affronted.

"I know you're not the owner," she said, staring him down, "because someone who owns a restaurant would never treat someone like that."

"I simply referred to monsieur's choice of clothing," he sniffed. "This is a very fine restaurant."

"I'll tell the owner you said that," Illyssa said flatly. "Where is he? I want to speak with him."

"Monsieur Voltaire is not here tonight," he said, beginning to look rather uncomfortable.

"I would like his phone number then," she said. "I think I should speak to him. If I had a restaurant, I would want to know if one of my employees were treating customers the way you do."

"Ha!" the man scoffed, trying to play the whole thing off as a joke, but quite aware that she meant business.

"Maybe you should show us to a table by the window," Illyssa said pleasantly. "Right away."

"Of course, mademoiselle," he said politely, with a smile no less.

After we were seated, the waiter informed us that Monsieur Maître d' would like to buy us a bottle of wine.

When we were alone, I whispered, "That was cool."

Illyssa treated the whole thing with nonchalance, but did explain gently, "You don't ever have to let someone treat you like that."

"This is a fancy place, though," I said in defense of my tormentor. "I should have worn a tie. You told me to wear a tie."

"I didn't tell you you should," she reminded me. "I said you might want to. That you didn't is perfectly fine. Don't worry about that. And this place isn't so fancy. That guy's not even French."

"How do you know that?" I said, mystified.

"I just know," she said with a shrug.

When I used the bathroom later in the night, the attendant confirmed for me that, in fact, the maître d' was from New Jersey.

How could I not be in love with a girl like that? She was the perfect paradox: demure but bold, soft but strong, quiet but opinionated, confident but humble, passionate but prudish. I thought Illyssa Wolkoff was the most beautiful human being ever to walk the earth. I was still intent on finding my mother and succeeding in the NFL, but my consciousness seemed to have suddenly sponged up some liquid calm. If all else failed me, there was someone of great substance and attractiveness who cared about me and loved me, maybe even adored me, no matter what had come before.

Fourteen

It was fortunate that I had Illyssa in my life. In the next several months, the clouds of uncertainty that filled the sky of my NFL career turned into a raging tempest. After a month of workouts, I returned to Syracuse for the summer, where I stayed with my parents. Despite my show of good faith, the general manager of the Falcons showed why he was one of the worst managers in the league by offering me a contract that was insulting. Although it was a deal for $900,000 over four years (more than my dad and mom had made together in their lives), it was pitifully low. The player chosen one pick ahead of me by Seattle got $1.6 million for four years. The player chosen after me got $1.35 million. Everyone knew that my contract had to fall somewhere between the two or me and my agent would be laughed at. I was about ready to take the money and run, but John wasn't going to be laughed at.

"If you want to take that money," he told me, "I'll have to resign as your agent. I couldn't let a client of mine sign a deal as blatantly bad as that."

Illyssa agreed with John. We were together on a vacation at Cape Cod with Stu and Colleen (they loved her, too).

"They'll get you as cheap as they can," she said. "This is business."

"But it's supposed to be about football," I complained. "I want to get down there and play. Training camp starts next week."

"It's business," she said flatly. "Get what you deserve."

"That's what John keeps telling me."

"John's right."

The local newspaper ran a story every week about my holdout, hinting that I had suddenly turned from the All-American hometown sports hero into a greedy glutton for money.

"Jealousy," Illyssa said over the phone. She had gone back to Long Island after Cape Cod.

Three weeks after the rest of my teammates had already begun training camp, I finally signed a deal—$1.45 million over four years. I returned to Atlanta to do what I'd always dreamed of doing: playing football for money, getting rich for playing a game. It turned out to be more difficult than it sounds. Life in the NFL was entirely different from college. Stepping out onto those fields was like stepping out into the center lane of a busy interstate. The size and speed of the bodies moving at and around me was overwhelming.

Camp made hell seem like a holiday. It was so hot, I couldn't hold onto my helmet when I took it off my head at the end of practice. When the coaches weren't running us, we were pounding each other mercilessly during drills that seemed to have no end. Every day was like two, with a practice in the morning and another one in the afternoon. During our free hour after lunch, I'd fall into an exhausted coma of sleep. Every waking moment was filled with physical pain. Muscles and joints were throbbing, my head was swollen two hat sizes from all the hitting, and I had to grease my forehead just to get my helmet back on before each practice. Despite three or four Tylenols every four hours, my head pounded as if it were caught in the doors of an elevator. Within a week, I began to assimilate, but on the tenth day, I tore my calf muscle. That injury would hobble me for more than a month and begin a series of ill-fated injuries that turned me from a bright and highly paid prospect into a marked man. In the NFL, there is no detraction quite so bad as when you are considered prone to injury.

Illyssa was back at Syracuse finishing up her last year of school. I took an apartment in Atlanta that I soon shared with fellow linebacker Joe Costello, who was picked up to replace the hole I had left in the roster. Coaches and teammates, the men I went to work with every day, were caught up in the winning of football games. Since, for the time being, I wasn't a part of it all, I turned into a kind of ghost. Except when I was in the training room getting therapy, my name was rarely spoken. I wasn't involved in the discussions of how we were going to blitz the 49ers or stop the Rams' running game. I was relegated to the sideline during practice, where I distracted myself by daydreaming on my crutches. In meetings, I hid in the darkest corners of the room and tried not to fall asleep.

During that frustrating rookie season I received—forwarded through my agent—a packet from the state of New York. I don't know if the information I received from the state was a good thing or a bad thing. It certainly spurred me on like a vicious kick underneath the ribs. It made my mother incredibly tangible. It was a line sketch that I filled in and shaded, creating a three-dimensional image that suited my most fantastic hopes and dreams. It was the nonidentifying information.

My mother, it said, was a college graduate who gave birth to me seven months after receiving her degree as a teacher. She had blue eyes, stood 5'6" tall, and weighed 140 pounds. She had apparently worked her way through school and enjoyed painting and sewing in her spare time. She was a Protestant, raised by her mother and her Irish father. Her father had been a professional baseball player who, upon retirement, was a member of the police force until his untimely death in an automobile accident while my mother was still a young girl.

Strangely, the information also told me that my mother had been married in the eighth month of her pregnancy to a man who was a longtime friend and not my father. As for my father's part, it merely said that he was 6'6" tall with hazel eyes, had a degree in mathematics, was of German decent, was raised as a Roman Catholic, and was in the military at the time of my birth.

I read and reread this information countless times. I kept it in a manila envelope on the dresser next to my bed. As I bubbled in the Falcons' hot tub or frittered away my time on crutches in the afternoon watching my teammates toil in the heat, I played each detail over and over again in my mind. I now knew vaguely what my mother looked like and who she was. As for my father, I had nothing more than a thumbnail impression. Still, it was easy for my imagination to fill in the rest, bringing their portraits to life with only slight departures from my previous daydreams.

I envisioned my mother as the daughter of some betrayed noble family who had the fortitude to make her own way despite a change in family fortunes. As for my father, the obvious thing was that he never knew about me. In the midst of a torrid love affair, his honor called him to defend his country. I presumed that he died a heroic death in Vietnam, probably never knowing of my existence. For my mother's part, I could envision my father's unscrupulous parents rejecting her and her unborn child simply because of the calamitous fall from society that had occasioned her once respected family. In a time when bearing an illegitimate child would have only heightened my mother's desperation, she was forced to give me up in the interest of my happiness.

They sound like silly schoolgirl dreams lifted from the pages of a Harlequin romance, but I never read a Harlequin romance, and no one ever knew I had these thoughts. No one even suspected. I was an NFL player, tough and mean, built up like a marble statue, cavalier and confident, a man's man. I guess I was those things, but at the same time, of course, I was still the boy who would cry himself to sleep over the tragic ending of a book.

Fifteen

My first NFL season ended, mercifully, with me starting in the final game and leading the team in tackles. Although it was my first start all year, it left the coaches with a good impression. It looked like my NFL career was back on track. Illyssa and I had kept in constant contact, visiting each other whenever the opportunity arose and speaking on the phone almost daily. In January, I went back to Syracuse and moved into the apartment of a friend, Ron Osinski, who had been one of my high school football coaches. I began working at the local NBC affiliate doing sports segments for the evening news in hopes of someday getting a job in network sports. I kept in shape by lifting and running at the university, and my relationship with Illyssa continued to flourish. Everything seemed to be right. Even my brother Kyle had what looked to be the perfect situation: a car (the one I'd given him), an apartment, and a job. My agent's partner in Chicago owned a construction company as well as several apartment buildings. Kyle was set up. He worked construction during the day. One of the apartment units owned by my agent came with the job. Not bad.

Armed with the nonidentifying information the state had given me, Doyle, my detective, set to work. The idea was that there couldn't have been that many policemen killed in automobile accidents who had also been professional baseball players. Several thousand dollars later, he came up with something. A cop from the nearby Utica

Police Force had been killed in a car wreck in 1956. This same cop, officer John Riggs, was once a member of a triple A baseball team, a kind of semipro player. It seemed an unusual set of circumstances that could be just the match for my mother's father. Doyle had used up all his retainer, but with just one more check he could play out this lead. To soften the blow of needing more money, Doyle then tossed in a prime tidbit. The obituary he found on Riggs said he was survived by a wife and a daughter. With a bit more money, he could search into the background of Officer Riggs and find out the identity of the daughter. I mailed out a check and waited.

While I waited, Kyle disappeared. My agent's partner told me that he had stopped going to work several weeks ago. Finally, the partner went to Kyle's apartment and found everything had been moved out. No one had heard from him and no one knew where he was. I called some of his old drug friends from Liverpool, but no one had a clue.

This frustrated me more than anything else. Kyle was a survivor, so I wasn't really worried about his safety. Sooner or later, he would turn up somewhere. It angered me, though, that I had established him in such a good situation only to have him pull up stakes without a word of explanation to anyone. There was no way then I could have known that it would be more than a year before I'd see my brother again, and no way to imagine the circumstances under which I would find him.

A few days after Kyle disappeared, I received the clipping from the old newspaper where Doyle had found the story on the man we thought might be my grandfather. Of course, the first person I wanted to show it to was Illyssa. She was in class until later in the afternoon, so I headed for the university field house to get my workout in. I was still welcome there, not only because I had only recently graduated but because the weight coach, Mike Woicik, was one of my dearest friends. Even though Mike had the responsibility for training every athlete at Syracuse University, he still took the time to train me one-on-one. That meant sweat and pain. After a lift that left my limbs quivering and numb, I ran a couple of miles and then threw myself down on the locker room floor. I was slick with sweat and drawing painful breaths that shook my ribs. The floor was dirty, but the cool air from the vent above chilled my wet skin and gave me new life.

On the other side of a blue metal door was the equipment room. From that room I heard boxes being dragged across a cement floor and slashed open with a razor. I reacted to that sound the way a dog will when it hears the rattle of food being poured into his dish.

I gathered my wind and bellowed through the door, "Mike! You've got some stuff! Hook me up, man!"

As equipment man, Mike was used to unequaled popularity among the athletes. During college, the NCAA used to forbid scholarship athletes to have a job while school was in session. Since the Syracuse athletic program wasn't crooked, we football players were almost always short on cash. As a result, athletic gear made up almost half of everybody's wardrobe. Even though I now had enough money to buy my own sneakers, sweatshirts, T-shirts, and shorts, out of habit I wanted some of the stuff Mike had for free.

The knob rattled and the door flew open. There was big jolly Mike, testing the limits of a pair of triple-X shorts and a double-X T-shirt. His white tube socks were pulled up to his knees. Behind him stood a troop of freshly delivered boxes, half of which were open and spilling valuable booty out onto the floor.

"I just saw the NFL schedule," Mike announced. "You guys are going to get your asses kicked by Miami. Marino is going to slaughter your secondary."

Mike was an inveterate Miami Dolphins fan.

"Yeah," I said, capitulating for the sake of some free stuff and because he was probably right. "They're looking good."

"Ha! Damn right they are!" he chortled.

"How about some stuff?" I said.

"You guys, you get to the NFL, and you still want hookups."

"I got you that Falcons hat," I reminded him, pointing to the wall inside the equipment room that was adorned with Mike's prodigious hat collection.

"Yeah," he said pensively, "you did. What do you want?"

"What do you have there?"

"I got T-shirts, sweat suits, some good stuff. How about one of each?"

I licked half a dozen beads of sweat from my upper lip and rose to my feet.

"Perfect," I said.

I stood in the doorway while Mike doled out the gear like Santa, filling my arms.

"You're the man, Mike," I told him.

"Marino's the man," he reminded me.

"Yeah. Hey, Mike, do you think I could have another one of those T-shirts?"

"Man . . . "

"For a kid," I said quickly.

"A kid?" Kyle said, arching his eyebrow. "Sure."

The shirt flew at me from across the equipment room and landed softly on top of the rest of my stuff.

"You and Marino, you're both huge," I said with a wink, then hit the showers.

Illyssa was back from her classes. I showed her the article Doyle had sent.

"Great," she said.

"This could be it," I told her.

"Maybe," she said uncertainly.

"Why do you say?"

"No, this could be it," she said. "If this isn't, it'll be something else."

"You think I'll find her?" I said.

"You will find her," she told me. "That's how you are."

"Maybe I already did," I said, waving the clipping.

I suggested dinner, and we climbed into my truck. Illyssa saw the stuff right off.

"Can I have this?" she asked, lifting the sweatshirt off the floor.

"Yeah," I said. "I'll share it with you."

"Wow, you got two T-shirts." Her voice was laced with the respect any knowledgeable college student gives to official athletic gear. "Can I send them to my brother?"

I shook my head, sorry to disappoint her.

"I need one of them," I told her. "You can send him mine, but I need one of them."

"For who?" she said casually.

"A kid," I told her.

"Oh," she said, brightening. "Who?"

"You know my grandparents," I began.

She nodded as I drove up to a little Italian restaurant and got out. She'd met them on several occasions. She loved my grandparents, two unassuming country folk in their seventies who still held hands.

"Well," I continued, opening her door and helping her down, "every Friday they volunteer at this hospital, you know, doing errands, delivering prescriptions, visiting with sick people."

We walked into the restaurant and got a table in the back corner. The light was dim but cheerful and the soft clinking of silverware and plates pinged quietly behind the symphony of fifty people talking at the same time.

"So one day a couple of years ago, they call and ask me if I would meet this little kid for lunch," I said, continuing my story. "Hell, it was the middle of football season, and it's the last thing I want to do, you know? I mean, between school and the season, but it's my grandparents, and they tell me that this little kid thinks I'm the greatest thing going. They knew his mom from the hospital. She's some nurse there, I guess. . . . "

Our waitress came up, told us the specials, and left us alone with two menus and a red plastic basket of bread that was warm enough to smell.

"My grandparents told me that the mom went through this really bad divorce," I said as I forced cold chunks of butter onto my bread, "and that they don't really have that much money. I guess the kid was taking it hard, you know. He missed his dad a lot, but he had this thing about me, you know, All-American football player and all that. . . . They tell me that the kid told his mom that the only thing he wants for Christmas is to meet Tim Green. That's it, the only thing he wanted . . .

"So," I said, looking up from my mangled bread before taking a bite, "I say 'sure.' I'm not going to disappoint my grandparents and this kid. So I meet him and he's a really nice little guy. And that's it. But, you know, I just try to send something to him every once in a while. You know, nothing big. I just like to stay in touch."

"I think that's so nice," Illyssa told me. Her big green eyes were serious and pretty. "You're a good person, Tim," she told me, reaching her slender hand across the checkered table and squeezing mine.

Although I thought from the very beginning that someone like Illyssa would make the perfect wife, I was now pretty sure that there was no one else like her. If I wanted a wife "like her," it was Illyssa or no one.

"I try," I told her, knowing she wouldn't have anything to do with anyone who wasn't nice. "I do try."

Sixteen

I did everything I could to forget about Doyle's search. I threw myself into my training as an athlete and a future broadcaster. And every minute I wasn't busy, I found myself searching out Illyssa. Her company meant more to me than anyone else's. Her kindness and easygoing manner drew me in like some innate beacon. Although we had both agreed that we were friends more than anything and would date other people if we felt like it, that option became moot during the spring and summer of that year.

It wasn't too long before I heard back from Doyle. Officer Riggs's daughter, he learned, was born in 1952. She would have been eleven at the time of my birth. What appeared to have been an incredible find was nothing more than a dead end.

"Look," Doyle said despondently, "I'm really sorry it didn't turn out."

"Me, too," I said.

"Well . . ." he said.

"Well," I said back at him.

"I just don't really see where to go," he told me. "I mean, I've checked out all the obituaries and police records in the upstate area. I could start checking Buffalo next, I guess. I checked in Cooperstown last week at the Baseball Hall of Fame as well, you know, to see if they had any record of a ballplayer who went on to be a cop and died at an early age. While I was there, I looked around for other cities close to Syracuse. Buffalo had a triple A team back then, too. . . . "

I pondered that for a moment. The spirit of never quitting that I had learned from my parents as well as from spending so much time in athletics overcame me. There was always another contest to be played and won. How could I expect it to be that easy? Doyle had only checked Syracuse, Rochester, and Utica. It was certainly possible that my mother had come from farther away than that to have her baby. It made sense to just keep expanding the search. Eventually, we would find my grandfather, and from there my mother.

"Do you think this is the best way to find her?" I asked.

"It's really the only way we have," he told me. "The problem is this: Your grandfather could have played baseball anywhere, San Diego for instance. Then maybe he joined a police force in Ohio, where he was originally from. Then maybe your mother came to Syracuse to have you. The possibilities are pretty limitless. I'm just hoping that maybe her dad stayed in the town that he played in and that she didn't travel far from home to have you. I think it's likely, but like I said, almost anything is possible. . . . "

I suspected from Doyle's tone that he had picked up some other work elsewhere, like he'd lost some enthusiasm somewhere along the way. Maybe he had some rich lady who wanted her husband spied on. Maybe that was how private eyes worked. I wanted him to check Buffalo though. I had a good feeling about Buffalo. It made sense. It wasn't too far, yet it wasn't close enough to home so that my mother would have had to worry about the scandal of bearing an illegitimate child.

"Well, let's check out Buffalo," I told him enthusiastically.

"Okay," he said, "I'll get on it."

"Good."

"Umm . . . "

"Yeah?"

"I know you don't want to hear this, but I've got to tell you. I think the best way to go about this is going to be to register with the state. Your mother may be on that registry and then you could find her without spending any more money. . . . "

"I really don't want to ask my parents," I said. "I still don't."

"I just think it's something that you might want to consider," Doyle said. "I think your parents would understand. . . . I'm just pointing out the option."

"Let's just go ahead with Buffalo," I said. "I've got a feeling about Buffalo."

Doyle sighed lightly, "Okay, I'll get back to you."

"When do you think?"

"Give me a month."

I didn't like Doyle pushing me toward the registry. He knew I didn't want to involve my parents. But the truth was, Doyle was right. I might be going through a lot of trouble for nothing. My mother might be out there, having registered with the state, hoping that I would do the same. She might be somewhere brooding away, because she had no idea how or where I was. She might be totally convinced that I wanted nothing to do with her, that I was enraged at her abandoning me and disinterested in registering with the state so that she could find me. That certainly wasn't true.

I thought about Buffalo instead. If something didn't turn up in Buffalo, maybe then I'd consider talking to my parents. Still, I couldn't shake the feeling that Buffalo was the place.

Seventeen

That summer I worked hard training for my second NFL season, running until I was sick and lifting weights until I collapsed. The enjoyable part of the summer was cultivating my relationship with Illyssa. She was easy to please. If I got her flowers, she was happy for a week. When I held her hand across the table during dinner, she beamed and told me how nice I was. But I did those things without thinking. I wanted to show her how much I cared and how much I thought of her as a person. I wanted to be a consummate gentleman like the characters created by Charles Dickens or Jane Austen. Illyssa, to me, was cut from the mold of their heroines.

There was only one time I acted the part of the villain, a disastrous and mistaken night with Beth. Even then, I hoped Illyssa would never find out. The last thing I wanted to do was hurt her, but on that one night, something small and selfish inside me won out.

Before I knew it, I heard from Doyle. Buffalo was a bust, and it was time to either ante up with another check or try something else. I told Illyssa the whole story and asked her what she thought about the registry.

"How bad do you want to know?" she asked.

"It's not a matter of how bad," I told her. "I have to find her. I can't think about not finding her. . . . "

Illyssa nodded.

"What about your parents?"

"That's the problem," I said. "I don't want to hurt them."

"That's what I was thinking. They were the ones who were there for you."

"I know that," I huffed. "That's not what this is about."

"I know," she said, "but I think they'll feel bad. I don't know. I don't know them as well as you. But you have to be careful."

"Sometimes if you want to get something, you can't just be careful," I told her.

"Sometimes," she told me, "when you get what *you* want, other people get hurt."

I pursed my lips and frowned. One thing I knew about Illyssa was that she would tell me what she thought, which was not necessarily what I wanted to hear. In that way, she was—and is—an invaluable ally.

"But," she conceded, "you have to do what your heart tells you. I think if it was me, I'd want to know, too. I think for you it's something you have to do."

Illyssa already knew that I usually ended up doing pretty much what I wanted anyway. Unless it was something egregious, she'd back me all the way.

"I love you," I told her.

"I love you, too," she said as simply as if she were saying "hello."

"Do you think I'll find her?"

"You will," she said. "If it's not this way, it'll be another, but you will."

Illyssa's words of caution made me reconsider going to my parents right way. There was still one thing I hadn't tried. The article that I found tucked away in my parent's papers two years before contained the name of the agency that had handled my adoption. It was called City of Syracuse Family Services. I looked it up in the phone book and made a call. I inquired as to who the director of the center was and if I could speak with her. I told the woman who answered the phone who I was, using my credentials as a former star football player at the university to get me past the director's buffer zone. It worked like a greased gear.

"This is Evelyn," the director said in an authoritative voice.

"Evelyn, I'm Tim Green," I explained, "the SU football player."

"Yes, I know," she said pleasantly. "How can I help you?"

"Well," I said, taking a deep breath to muster all the pleasantry I had at my disposal, "I was adopted, and your agency handled my adoption when I was only a couple of months old. I wanted to try to sit down and talk with you about some things. I'm trying to find my mother. . . . "

Evelyn's voice got frosty. "I can't really help you with anything," she told me. "Your records are with the state, and I have no access to them."

"I know. I know," I said hurriedly, wanting to get past the chill. "I just wanted to sit down and talk with you . . . see the place. You know, just to get a feel for the whole thing. I think I may have been there when I was really young, to pick up my brother. He was adopted, too. Would you mind if I stopped by?"

I knew from experience that while my name could get the director on the phone, my presence was a lot more likely to get her to say yes to helping me than my voice. In person, I could always get more. If I got to see her face-to-face, I could go to work again, right from the start. Who could say? I might even bump into someone else in the office who would be willing to help me.

Two days later, when I arrived, I was struck with the austerity of the place, nothing more than another low-level county government office. The carpet was well-worn and the color of faded mustard. The furniture was cheap and musty. The magazines in the waiting area were dog-eared, at least three months old. My presence seemed to send at least a few of the girls behind the sliding glass partition into a tizzy, and even Evelyn herself seemed nervous and self-conscious as she showed me into a tiny conference room in the back. I was all smiles and cheery hellos. I wanted to charm every single one of them, hoping that some clandestine phone call might follow in a few days when one of them became overwhelmed with sympathy for my plight: a man separated from his mother at birth, a man desperate to find her and share some of his good fortune.

Evelyn told me about the role the agency played in people's adoptions and how the state carefully guarded the information of each case in its records bureau in Albany. She assured me that there was no way she could be of any service to me, other than to let me know that everything her office did, they did by the book. I pressed her. I had the feeling that although there was nothing she could do as far as unearthing my records, there was something she wanted to tell me, something she knew that could help me. It was a feeling, but I knew from being around Illyssa that I should follow those kinds of feelings. Often they are correct.

"Please," I said quietly and with real emotion, "I need help. . . . "

Evelyn pursed her lips and looked down at her hands. The fingers of one hand were gripped tightly in the other. Her lips began to work, but no words came out.

"I can't tell you," she said finally, shaking her head resolutely. "I'm sorry."

I knew that was the end. I had come to the precipice of knowing something, but now I was being turned back. I can't express the feeling of sadness and rage I felt. I wanted to shake her. I could only see another human being in front of me, refusing to help me in my quest because of rules written on lifeless paper, generated in offices like the one we were sitting in by people who had no real connection to what I was going through. It was heartless and wrong. How could they keep me separated from her? What right did they have?

I contained my rage, however, knowing that a burned bridge could never help this cause or any other.

"Okay," I said getting up. I forced a smile and extended my hand. "Thank you, anyway. If something ever changes, please call me."

I walked out of there, sick not only from my failure but from the knowledge of what I now had to do.

Eighteen

My father worked in downtown Syracuse at the ornate art deco building of the regional power company. I picked him up in my truck one day that summer around noon. I drove him to one of my favorite restaurants for a really good lunch. We hadn't gotten past the hostess's station before the owner began fussing. He was a huge Syracuse football fan and delighted, he said, to meet my father. This was pleasing. I wanted to make it clear to my dad that I was proud of him and that he was part of all the good things that had happened to me. We had lunch, and I rattled off all the latest news I could think of about the NFL and how I had been preparing for the upcoming season. I ate without tasting anything. Every time I felt like there was an opening to broach the subject, my eyes started to well up with tears and I retreated to my banter.

My father, being the pleasant, easygoing man that he is, never suspected that something was boiling inside of me. He didn't notice the high-pitched break from time to time in my nervous laugh or the way my hand shook ever so slightly, gently rattling the cubes of ice on the inside of my water glass every time I took a drink to ease my constricted throat. My dad just sat and beamed at the gossip I could relate to him as a true NFL insider.

We were at the traffic light one block from my dad's office, and I was safe behind a pair of sunglasses when I suddenly turned down the radio and blurted out, "Dad, I want to tell you something. I mean, I want to ask you something."

"Okay," he said, his voice strained by the abruptness of my words and the enigmatic tone of my voice.

"I don't want to hurt you or Mom, you know that. I . . . there's something I've been kind of wondering about for a while, not because you guys aren't great parents . . . "

I pulled up alongside his silver-gilded building and stopped talking. I wanted him to get it and just say okay. I wanted him to decipher what I was saying and make it easy, but how could he have known what I was talking about?

I took a long deep breath through my nose and then told my father the story of Beth's mother the way it was related to me almost two years before.

"Somewhere out there," I concluded, "there's a woman who has no idea what happened to me. I want her to know that everything worked out great, that I'm happy. I don't want her to not know. Everything has turned out . . . so well. . . . "

"Well, I think that's great," my father said without hesitation. "I think I'd want to do the same thing if I were you."

"You don't feel bad?" I said, unable to hide my surprise. "I mean, I don't want you guys to think that I don't love you and that you haven't been great parents. I don't want Mom to feel bad."

"I can't imagine she would," my father replied. "I think it's only natural that you'd want to know."

"I want to let her know," I reminded him.

"Yes, well, I think you'd want to know, too," he said gently.

"I'm so glad you feel this way. Do you think Mom will be okay?"

"Of course, she'll be fine."

"Will you tell her? I mean, I need to get you guys to sign a waiver before I can get any kind of information. If my biological mother has registered and I get you guys to sign off, I'll know."

"What if she hasn't registered?" my father asked.

I thought about that. I was certain that she had. After all, she was my mother. If she was the woman I thought she was, she had probably conducted an exhausting search to find me—the way Audry had searched for her son—to make sure everything had turned out all right.

"I don't know," I said. "If she hasn't, then I don't know. . . . "

"Well, just don't get your hopes up," my father said in his usual way, as if he were talking about making the varsity football team as a freshman.

"But you'll talk to Mom about it?" I said, discounting his caution. "I was thinking I could bring the papers by later this week."

"I'll tell her, but don't worry. She'll be fine."

"Dad," I said, holding out my cold sweaty hand, "thanks. I love you."

When my father got out of the car, I had the distinct sensation of having held my head too close to the muzzle of a discharged firearm. Everything was ringing. I don't know how I got back to my apartment, but I did. As I walked up the driveway toward the front door, I realized that I felt much lighter. In fact, I seemed to float.

Later that week, I crossed the streets that marked the boundaries of my old neighborhood. Illyssa rode shotgun. We passed the elementary school where I had learned to read and where my mother still taught fourth grade. The houses and streets and yards were as familiar to me as the inside of my own bedroom closet. I had walked every inch of them over and over as a kid, if not when visiting my friends then when delivering newspapers for $11 a week.

We passed by the green area and I thought of the countless hours I spent with my own dog, trudging through winter nights when I could see nothing beyond the swirling snow and imagining the collie was a wolf and that she and I were in Alaska or some other faraway place. I turned down Kiwi Path, remembering it not as my street but as the final stretch of the two-mile run I must have taken a thousand times. We passed by my old neighbors' homes. I tried to tally up the hours I'd spent cutting their lawns in the summer and shoveling out their driveways in the winter. I wanted to think about everything except why I was coming home.

My own house sat at the end of the street on the corner, and I somehow felt that I belonged anywhere else but there. Beside me on the console between Illyssa's seat and mine were the papers that I needed in order to find my mother. I came to the end of the street, rounded the corner, and immediately ascended our steep driveway, the perfect place for the entire neighborhood to go sledding in the winter and skateboarding in the summer. Even though we were all grown up, the kids still came.

I shut off the engine and sat a moment, unable to shake the feeling that I was like some shyster bagging a middle-aged couple in a Ponzi scheme. It was a done deal. My father told me over the phone that he had spoken with my mother and everything was all set. I would walk in there, get them to sign on the dotted line, and meet my objective. But I would leave them barren, the victims of a vile scam. By signing these papers, they were allowing someone else to come in, another person or persons who hadn't lifted a finger for me to call themselves my parents. It was robbery.

"Are you okay?" Illyssa asked.

I nodded.

"Are you sure?" she said, allowing her hand to rest on my knee.

"Yeah," I said, and got out of the truck.

We walked into the garage and opened the door that led to the house. The distinct and familiar screech of unoiled hinges welcomed me like an old friend. I could smell the rich buttery scent of cookies cooling on a rack beside the oven. My parents had put down a new carpet in the family room since my last visit, but the dark paneled walls and the arrangement of the furniture remained the same as it always had been and as it always will be. Everything looked slightly smaller to me, though. It wasn't that I was bigger, it was because, in my mind, the world around me was expanding rapidly. I lived in Atlanta, and as a pro, I traveled on a weekly basis to cities like Chicago, L.A., and New York. We stayed in skyscrapers and played in colossal stadiums. The house I grew up in, however, had stayed the same.

The living room opened to the kitchen, which was demarcated by three steps up and a long decorative cast-iron railing. My parents were at the table with hot cups of coffee. I greeted them, and Illyssa and I sat down. We talked small for a few minutes. Tension arced between us like blue electricity. Illyssa stayed mostly quiet, but held my hand tightly underneath the table. We all knew why I was there. None of us really wanted to talk about that.

"Well," I finally said, bringing the papers forth from my lap and laying them on the table.

"Yes," my father said, congenially picking up the pen and flourishing his name.

He pushed the document across the table to my mother. She sniffed distastefully and pushed her glasses up higher on her nose.

"I guess I have Audry to thank for this," she said, unable to help herself, tears welling.

"Mom . . ."

She held the papers at arm's length to better scrutinize them.

"I want to know what it is I'm signing," she explained hotly.

I gave my father an "I-told-you-so" look. He pretended not to see me.

"Come on, Judy," he said, "we know what it is."

"This wasn't supposed to be like this," she said, straightening her back and pushing the papers back toward me ever so slightly. "We had an agreement. We all signed things years ago, legal things. This wasn't supposed to happen."

I could have explained. I could have apologized and gone away. If I backed down now, the hurt would heal. The fact that I wanted to find another woman who could call herself my mother was forgivable. If I left now, my mother, Judy, could write that off as a nefarious curiosity, like wondering what it would feel like to jump off a building. It was the act that would be unforgettable. To her, the act of finding my biological mother could rob her of something she'd worked twenty-three years for, and something she was terribly proud to call her own: her son.

She had worked for me. She worked around our house to keep it clean and nice. She had toiled away as a teacher so we could have money to go on vacations, send us to summer camp, and buy a new television when the old one wore out. She had cleaned my practice gear, mended my uniforms, made my enormous lunches, and nursed me back to health through injury as well as sickness. After all her efforts, this was to be her thanks: I would look for the only other woman who could lay claim to her title without lifting a finger.

"You said you'd sign it," I told her.

"I will," my mother replied with an indignant scowl as she picked up the pen. "I just want you to know that this wasn't supposed to happen."

And she was right. When they'd adopted me twenty-three years before, they were assured that all bonds between me and my biological parents were severed. That was part of the deal. I was theirs and no one else's. It was legal and binding. No one back then told them about a registry. I was forcing them to allow a promise made to them years ago to be broken. While I was indignant about having the identity of my biological mother kept from me, how indignant must they have felt in having that guarantee voided?

For my father, it was matter of logic. He understood why I was curious. It made sense to him. I was born. I was given up for adoption. I had innate characteristics that were inexplicable. The biological link to my mother could help to explain some of the questions I had about myself. My father's job was about making sense of things, designing computer programs constructed entirely on logic, and I think he often applied the same principles to life. But for my mother it was different, and I think every mother will tell you that it just is.

I knew this about my mother. I knew from her words, from her body language, and from the quavering tone of her voice the impact this event was having on her. It was as though I had brought her to the brink of that same chasm I had dreamed about so many times in my nightmares. It was as if I were standing behind her as she teetered, and if I moved that paper just an inch, it would tilt the balance. She would fall. I looked at Illyssa. She watched with horror. I looked at my father. He blinked.

Yes, I felt horrible, but I pushed that paper back toward my mother, not even an inch. Her eyes brimmed with tears, but she gave one final nod and then signed it. Though sick with myself, I managed to choke out a thank-you. We tried to lapse back into the narcotic comfort of small talk, but we could no more return to normal than could a village razed by napalm be rebuilt to look the same way it had before the destruction. I came up with some inane excuse about how we had to get going, took Illyssa by the hand, and drove out of my old neighborhood feeling no better than a criminal with a conscience. I had delivered a blow, unaware of its impact. The crack I put in our relationship would gradually widen into a fissure. I never imagined how much I would have to change and how many years would pass before I could bridge that gap.

Nineteen

It was during the summer when I filed with the state adoption registry that I also became a writer. I had written before. During my studies as an English major at Syracuse University, I had taken several creative writing classes. But until that time I had only written short stories. My dream, since early on, was to become a novelist, to enchant people with compelling tales and transport them into other worlds as perfectly as Alexandre Dumas, Ernest Hemingway, and Charles Dickens had transported me.

I think I wanted to write for several reasons. First, I loved to read and therefore admired writing. Second, if I could actually become an author, it would give people one more reason to admire *me*, a need whose origins I've already discussed. Books were revered in our household while I was growing up, and I knew that the author of such a thing would be duly venerated. And I think that we all have a basic longing for immortality. I know I do, and writing a book seems to be as good as any other method of achieving that. From my experiences as an English major, I know that at least a part of the spirit of men and women who have expired long ago still live on in the books they wrote.

The problem for me up until that point in my life had been the daunting amount of time and energy I knew it would take to write a book, let alone the skill. But something inspired me that summer. Maybe it was the desperate need to earn one more badge of honor, to give my mother, if I could find her, one more reason to love and adore me. Maybe it was so that my own parents, despite their disappointment at my apostasy, might admire me still. Maybe I wanted to leave some imprint for posterity to prove that, in fact, I did exist, just in case I never found my past. Maybe I needed something to distract myself from the impending answer from the state, someplace to direct the rabid thoughts that would spring to life at every idle moment. Or quite possibly, and quite simply, it was because I was made to write and had finally matured to the point at which I had a story to tell and was ready to begin what would become a lifelong craft.

Whatever the reason, I went to the store and, knowing nothing about computers, bought a laptop model with a simple word-processing program. The only thing I knew less about than computers was typing, but I was determined to become proficient enough at both so that I could one day make a living as a writer. I reasoned that to write full-length novels without being able to type or use a computer was fool's work. And since I was serious about the business of writing, I went out and got a job as a weekly columnist for the Syracuse newspaper, reporting what my life in the NFL with the Atlanta Falcons was really like.

To deal with the onerous notion of actually writing four hundred pages, I decided that I would give myself four years in which to write my first book. That way, I would only have to produce two typed pages a week for my novel to stay on schedule. With football season and my novel under way, and with a weekly deadline for my column, there was very little time for pondering what the answer to my registration with the state adoption registry would bring.

At the end of that summer, Illyssa and I tried to convince ourselves that it would be best for her to develop real estate in her father's business in New York City. She was young, bright, and energetic. I would be busy enough for two in Atlanta. We could get together on weekends, we reasoned, from time to time. However, the reality was that we spent so much time and money on phone calls and flying her down to Atlanta whenever I had a spare minute that we decided the best thing to do was admit that we couldn't be apart.

Contentment for both of us was predicated on each other's presence. Illyssa's two-day weekends turned into three-day weekends, and then into four- or five-day weekends. Soon she was in Atlanta with me more than at the office with her new job. It was obvious we'd both be better off if she moved down for good. Together, we looked for a place to live and settled on a golf course condominium between Suwanee, where the Falcons facility was, and downtown Atlanta, where our favorite restaurants and theaters were.

Even though she was happy to be in Atlanta, Illyssa was somewhat uncomfortable if not outright suspicious about women I may have dated during the first year in Atlanta while she was still at school. Although we had talked openly about seeing other people that first year, now that I'd asked her to move in, it was an entirely different story.

"I don't want any more of that," she told me. "If you're with me, you're not with anyone else."

I agreed. Two weeks after moving into our new place, I got a letter from Beth. I had just returned to the condo from a long day of practice. I was exhausted and not ready for the drama about to unfold. While Illyssa hadn't opened the letter, she waited with high anxiety while I did so in front of her. What else could I do? To take the letter off to myself would have been to admit some kind of guilt. If I hadn't been so tired, I might have thought to simply throw the letter away, saying there wasn't anything Beth could say that I needed to hear.

I scanned the letter nervously. We were standing in the kitchen. There didn't seem to be anything incriminating in there at first blush, so with a nervous laugh I handed the letter over to Illyssa.

"It's no big deal," I explained. "You know, she wants to see me some time. I can't help that. . . . "

Illyssa said nothing. She was poring over that letter.

"You bastard," she said, slowly looking up at me.

My heart sank. My stomach churned.

"You saw her this summer," she seethed. "You told me you were over her. You told me and told me. I said you weren't. You bastard."

"Illyssa, I . . . "

"Don't you lie to me, you saw her!"

I hadn't read the letter carefully, but I knew it must be in there, some reference to the one time I had seen Beth that summer. Illyssa had been in New York. It really hadn't been anything, just my determination to go out on top, to be the rejecter rather than the rejected. To see her, be with her, then spurn her the way she had spurned me more than a year before. It was the same trick I had played on Kate, my high school girlfriend. But how could I explain to Illyssa the distracting and desperate need I had not to be rejected by a woman I loved? I didn't even realize myself why I'd done it, just that I had.

"Illyssa, it was just once. It didn't mean anything."

I knew the real problem wasn't that I'd been with another woman. Technically, I hadn't made the commitment to monogamy until Illyssa came to Atlanta. This happened before that. It was the who, not the what. Illyssa's biggest apprehension was that I would go back with Beth. Maybe she thought I couldn't live with the rejection, and if I had a chance to undo it, I would.

She lifted the letter and in a mock voice read, "'Hopefully, we can get together again soon.'. . . Is that your plan! You brought me down here for *this*!"

Then she was gone from the room. I followed her to the bedroom, where the door was promptly slammed in my face and the bolt thrown.

"Illyssa!" I begged. "Let me explain. It's nothing. It didn't mean anything!"

"You were going to see her *again*!" she screamed through the door. "I'm not staying here, Tim. I'm not living that way. I had that before. I'm not having that again!"

"Illyssa! Let me in! Let me talk to you!"

She refused to speak. Through the door, I could hear the opening and closing of dresser drawers and constant trips to and from the closet. At one point, I heard her muffled voice. She was speaking on the telephone. I picked the letter up off the floor and sat down on the couch to examine my error and suffer in silence. Not until I heard the horn of the cab out front did I fully realize how dearly one night with my ex-girlfriend was going to cost me.

She came streaking out of the bedroom with her suitcase in hand. I grabbed at her arm.

"Illyssa!"

"Don't you *touch* me!" she shrieked, snapping her arm away from me with strength I didn't even know she had.

"Illyssa," I moaned. My eyes were filling with tears. I walked along beside her out to the cab, pleading.

"Don't go, Illyssa. Don't go."

She pretended not to hear me. The driver, a young, overweight redneck with long hair, loaded her suitcase into the trunk with obvious embarrassment.

I stood there in the concrete driveway. The lush green trees towering above rustled in the warm breeze. The sky was clear and sharply blue. The sun was low but bright, a perfect day, except that she was gone. I stood there alone, chewing my lower lip, incensed with my stupidity at committing the act and getting caught. I deserved to be alone. That was my conclusion. I didn't merit a woman like Illyssa. Deep down there was something terribly wrong with me.

At age three,
my mom told
me I was special.

Waiting for the school bus,
I stood out because of my size.

At kindergarten,
I was quiet and introspective.

My older sister, Laurie, at eleven,
with me, six, and Kyle, three.

I wanted those merit badges!

My days were happy.
It was the nightmares
that scared me.

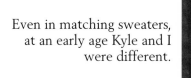

Even in matching sweaters,
at an early age Kyle and I
were different.

At age ten, giving my mom
her Christmas present. I
always wanted to please her.

We almost always got
what we wanted for
Christmas.

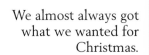

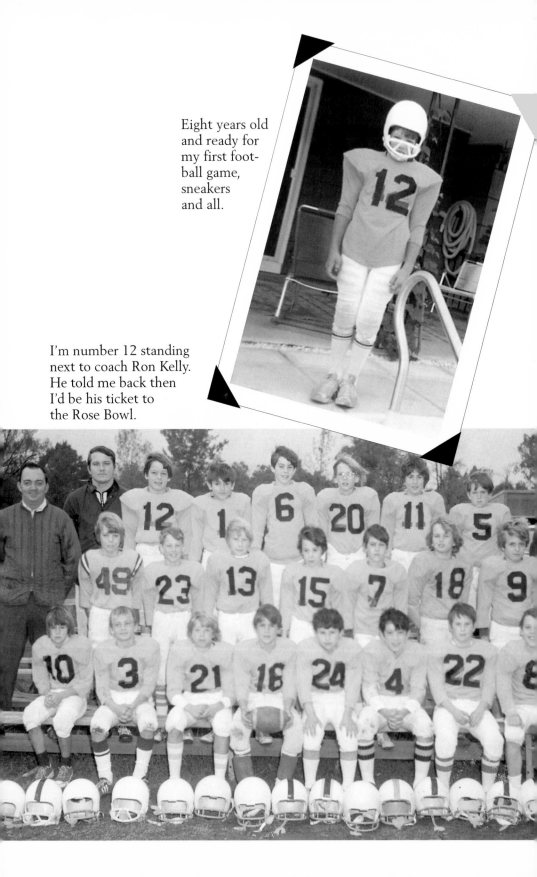

Eight years old and ready for my first football game, sneakers and all.

I'm number 12 standing next to coach Ron Kelly. He told me back then I'd be his ticket to the Rose Bowl.

Ready to make the move from
middle school to high school.
Now all I needed were some
contact lenses.
(Courtesy of Colleen Lisson)

The only sophomore on
the County All-Star team,
I still wasn't satisfied.
(Courtesy of Stu Lisson)

As a senior in high school, I took a gold medal
in wrestling at the Empire State Games. As
always, my family was there cheering me on.
(Courtesy of Sharon Fulmer)

Wrestling with a nasty attitude.
(Courtesy of Steve Parker)

My dad visiting the practice
field at Syracuse University.

I was smiling, but life as
an NFL rookie could be grueling.
(Courtesy of Jimmy Cribb)

From the day we met,
Illyssa and I seemed
to fit together.
(Courtesy of Stu Lisson)

A dramatic setting on the most important day of my life.

My dad and his boys.

My mother knew I was marrying the right woman.

My parents became
Falcons fans for life.

Kyle and I
having dinner
in Atlanta
during one
of his breaks
from the road.

I was my brother
Kenny's best man.

I can't get enough
of fatherhood!

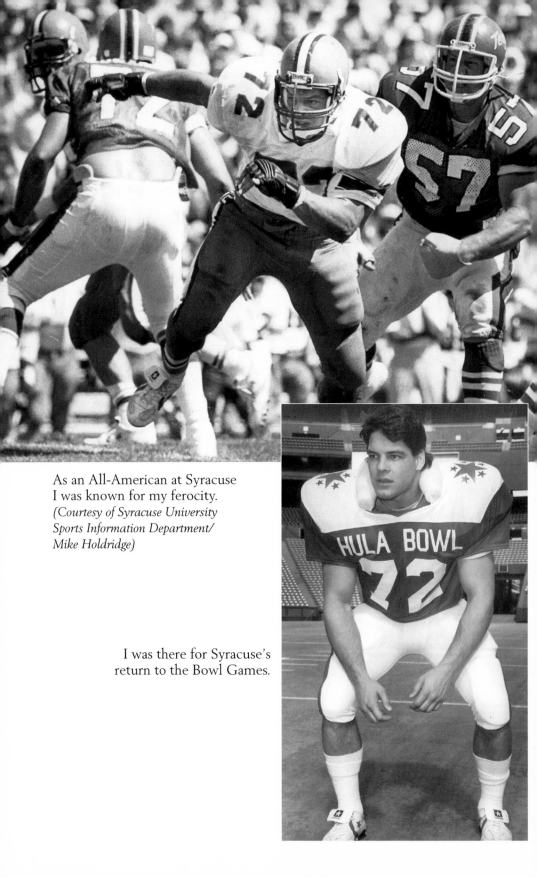

As an All-American at Syracuse
I was known for my ferocity.
*(Courtesy of Syracuse University
Sports Information Department/
Mike Holdridge)*

I was there for Syracuse's
return to the Bowl Games.

The rage and ferocity
of playing with the NFL.
(Courtesy of Jimmy Cribb)

My number one fan.
(Courtesy of Sharon Fulmer)

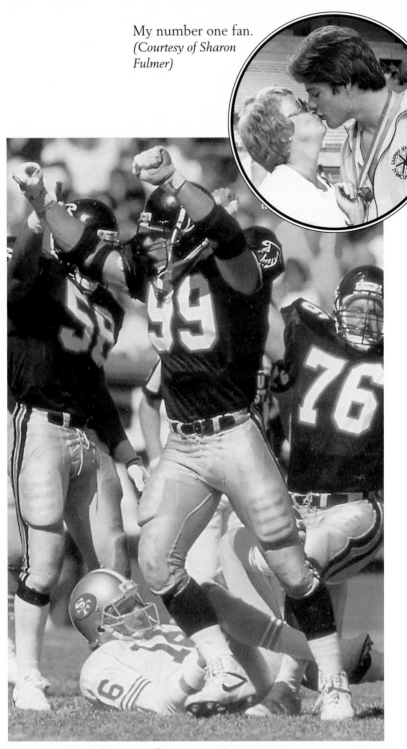

A celebration after pummeling Joe Montana.
(Courtesy of Jimmy Cribb)

Twenty

I had no choice but to stay in Atlanta. There was no way I could follow Illyssa. I had practice every day all week, and that Saturday we left for Los Angeles to play the Rams. It was as bad as any week of my life. Illyssa wouldn't take my calls at home or at her father's office. Her mother, like her father's secretary, was frosty and abrupt. By the end of the week, despise me as they may, I think even they admired my resolve. I called both her home and office four times a day, once in the morning, once at our lunch break, once right before practice, and once in the evening when I got home to my empty condo. I ate out every night and drank a lot of beer. Practices were miserable, because it was hot. I was hung over and despondent. The offensive linemen had a field day with me that week, punching me about on the field as if I were just another bright orange tackling dummy that couldn't hit back. The linebacker coach told me I'd better get my head out of my ass before we went to L.A. I didn't know if that was possible. I thought, under the circumstances, my head was right where it should have been.

We got home from L.A. late Sunday night, then had to watch game film and lift weights Monday morning, but we were done by noon. Tuesday was our day off, so by two o'clock Monday, I was on a plane for New York. I took a cab to her father's office and walked right in.

Everyone stopped working. It was just after five, but those who had been on their way out the door stopped to watch. The secretaries averted their eyes. The men stared through the doorways to their offices as I made my way toward the end of the building, where I knew her father's office was. I rounded a bend and saw her standing there with a file in her hand, talking to her father's secretary, who was seated at her desk.

I must have looked like hell. I was tired and hurt, physically as well as emotionally. My coach had been right, the Rams had had a field day with me. I was limping from a deep bruise I had in my thigh and a nasty gash ran from my eye to the corner of my mouth where someone's finger had gotten through my face mask during the game. Exhaustion had drawn heavy circles under my eyes.

"Please come back," I said. "I need you to come back. I'm sorry. Please."

Illyssa looked at the secretary, who got up and walked away. I took her hands in mine.

"I told you I wasn't going to be made a fool of," she said quietly. "I didn't go down there to have you run back to her. If you want her, you go have her. You want someone to treat you the way she did, fine. That's what you deserve. . . . "

"Illyssa, you can't leave me."

I was now crying like a fool.

"Listen, if I don't have you, I'm completely alone. Don't you understand? I don't have anyone, Illyssa. I don't know where I came from. I don't know who I'm a part of. I'm . . . totally disconnected. You're the first person that made me feel, deep down, like I really wasn't alone. The first. Please, I would never leave you for someone else, anyone else, you've got to know that. . . . "

She looked past me for a moment and with a look dispersed the people who had gathered to watch. Then she opened her arms and let me hold her close. I put my head on her shoulder and cried hard.

"I'm alone," I sobbed. "I'm so goddamned alone. . . . "

She took my face in her hands and held me in her gaze. "You're not alone," she said, and held me again. I knew deep down for the first time in my life that it was true.

Twenty-one

Illyssa came back and the football season progressed. We had a terrible team. All the hard work and physical pain it had taken to get to the NFL seemed at times a senseless waste while playing for the hapless Falcons. I learned a painful lesson: When you lose in the NFL, you might be better off, during the season at least, not to have played the game at all. Instead of adulation and city-wide respect, we Falcons were more familiar with derision and scorn. Pencil-necked radio DJs mocked us. Out-of-shape newspaper columnists called for our jobs. Neighbors snickered behind our backs.

Still, I went to practice, day after day, week after week, sweating, bleeding, and aching. At the end of the day, when Illyssa had finally gone to sleep and I was alone in the condominium we had taken to calling our home, I would write. Halfway through that miserable second NFL season, I returned home one balmy fall evening to find Illyssa disconcerted. She was on the phone when I walked in and I could tell by the way she shifted her eyes as she spoke that she had something to tell me. I had the sense she would rather have remained on the phone, talking until the end of time, than tell me whatever news it was she had to reveal.

Finally she hung up.

"What?" I said.

Her eyes misted over and I shifted my gaze instinctively past her to the cool green foliage of the seventh fairway resting just outside our back window. The serenity of the close-cut grass and the neatly trimmed shrubs created a nice mental cushion for the impact of whatever bad news she was about to drop. Illyssa, I could see, was on the verge of tears. She isn't the type of person to cry for herself. She's too tough. So I knew, whatever the reason, she was distraught for me.

"This came today," she told me, revealing a white envelope, already opened, from the state of New York.

I didn't move to take it from her. It hung between her fingers, suspended between us. Illyssa didn't have to tell me. I didn't have to read what was inside. I knew from her look that my mother hadn't registered with the state. I knew that this letter was going to tell me that they would not release the identifying information because she was not looking for me as ardently as I was looking for her.

"You'll find her," she said, subduing her emotions behind a high-held chin and a determined face.

I drew strength from her resolve, then averted my gaze again to the scenic view, afraid of the honest answer to my next question.

"You think I will?"

"Yes," she said, "I do. You'll find her. You will."

Illyssa, I already knew, was prophetic. When she said something was going to happen, I had come to expect that it would. She is somehow in touch with the energy of our universe in such a way that she really does sense whether or not things will happen. It is a mixed blessing, this gift of hers. But even then, I knew enough to trust her instincts, at least enough to allow hope to creep back into my mind after this savage blow.

The news behind the news, of course, was that my mother, wherever and whoever she was, did not have the same sense of urgency to find me as I had developed in trying to find her. Obviously, whatever her feelings, they weren't the same set of emotions that Audry had felt for the son she put up for adoption. Audry, I knew, had gone to great lengths, utilizing every means available to locate and identify the son she had borne and then given away.

In a way, I wasn't certain that I wanted Illyssa's prophecy to come true. Did I want to find my mother if she didn't want to be found? How could it be that she hadn't registered? Was she, in fact, not anything close to the image I had created of her in my mind? It was quite possible that I was setting myself up for the worst rejection of all: finding, only to have her send me away again. Two things enabled me to continue my search. One, it was possible that my mother didn't know about the registry, or that there was some other logical reason why she hadn't searched. Maybe she was afraid of how I might react to her. Maybe she felt she had forfeited the right to be a part of my life. Two, with Illyssa beside me, I knew I wasn't alone. I knew that no matter how it turned out with my mother, I had a woman I was physically connected with who would be there for me no matter what. If I couldn't have a past with my mother, I knew I would have a future with Illyssa.

Twenty-two

The football season in Atlanta ended with a pathetic final record of 3–13. I could be found during the final weeks in the hot tub, rehabilitating a torn ligament in my knee. Illyssa and I were thankful to free ourselves from the malaise of the Falcons and return to Syracuse, where I continued to work part-time in television and where Illyssa opened a bed-and-bath boutique in Armory Square, a revitalized downtown area of Syracuse. It was easy enough for both of us to stay busy, but still we devoted substantial efforts toward finding my biological mother. Within a month of returning home we learned from a friend who'd been watching *Oprah Winfrey* that not only was my situation quite common, but that there was an association called ALMA whose entire mission was reuniting children and parents separated at birth through adoption. ALMA not only lobbied on behalf of adopted people for legislative reform to loosen the legal restrictions on adoption information, but they had a registry of their own, in case children or parents either hadn't heard of the registry in their state or if they hailed from states where no such registry existed.

I joined ALMA and registered immediately. It didn't take long to learn that my mother hadn't registered with ALMA either. But besides the registry, the organization sent us information, as it does to all its members, suggesting methods for finding biological parents or children beyond the available registries. One idea that seemed to be a long shot, but one that was easy enough to undertake, was to take out a personal ad in the newspaper of the city in which you were born. Some parents and children, the information told us, had been reunited after years of frustrating search through the simple means of a personal ad. Of course, I couldn't help thinking that could happen to me.

The other thing I learned from the information I received from ALMA was that there was no one single way to find one's mother. The only universal quality shared by those who were successful in their quest was relentlessness. The way to succeed was to use every available means, and when you failed, to think of some other method. I couldn't imagine much beyond private detectives, registries, political favors, and personal ads, each of which I had either tried or was trying. If these failed me, I didn't know what else there was, and this feeling of helplessness prompted me to try and dilute the need to find my mother by occupying my mind with the other aspects of my life.

Just as they were during football season, my days were filled. Illyssa and I purchased a small two-bedroom duplex in Liverpool, not far from where I'd grown up. After breakfast, she'd head to her store and I'd go to the weight room, the track, and the karate dojo in order to stay in shape. Some days I'd work on a weekly sports talk show I was hosting at the local cable station. Evenings we'd spend together, either going out for dinner with friends, or renting movies and staying home on our couch. After our time together, I'd hammer away diligently on my computer, mindful of the writer I wanted to become. My desk was set up in an alcove immediately adjacent to our antique oak bed. It was common for Illyssa to wake up sometime in the middle of the night and urge me to come to bed. But with my novel beginning to take shape, it was not unusual at all for me to fall asleep propped up in front of my keyboard sometime after two or three in the morning.

Although I now lived only ten minutes from my parents' home, I seemed to be seeing them less than ever. It was as if an infection was festering beneath the surface of our relationship, but no one was willing, or able, to lance it. Dinners and holiday gatherings had begun to take on artificial tones, and more and more time went by between even the simplest of phone conversations. It seems logical to believe that what was happening was a combination of my parents' hurt and my own sense of guilt for the search I was conducting, although I must admit, this is only speculation. To this day my parents and I have never discussed that period of time. I doubt we ever will.

The incredible news came while I was out. Again, I knew something was happening before Illyssa said a word. I had returned from my typical day of workouts. Illyssa appeared anxious the moment I walked into the house and spoke even before I had a chance to drop my gym bag onto the table by the door.

"You got a call from the paper," she told me excitedly. "There's a woman who responded to the ad who says she's your mother."

"My God," I heard myself say.

"The person from the paper wouldn't give her our number, but he told her he'd contact you."

"So she doesn't know who I am?" I asked, my mind spinning.

"No, she just knows what was in the ad."

The only information in the ad had been my date of birth, my sex, my height and weight, and that I was born in the Syracuse area. The height and weight had come from the medical information I'd copied from my parent's papers two years before.

"So, she had a son born when I was born," I said.

"She says she's your mother," Illyssa said. "She wants to meet you. The man from the paper told me she'd be at The Varsity tomorrow at one o'clock. She told him she'd be wearing a sun hat and that she'd be sitting in a booth by herself."

My stomach seemed to be forcing itself up into my throat, threatening to spill its entire contents out of my mouth. I felt drunk. I reeled and sat down on the couch.

"I can't believe it," I said. "I found her."

I looked up at Illyssa and blinked.

"Can you?" I said.

"I don't know," she told me. "Let's see. I don't know . . . "

"What does that mean, you don't know?" I demanded, unable to hide my exasperation.

"Just wait and see," she told me. "I just don't want you to get too excited until you know . . . for sure."

"She answered the ad," I reminded her.

"I know."

"How could she not be?"

"Maybe she is."

I ate very little at dinner and tasted nothing. I laid down in bed with Illyssa but couldn't sleep. Over and over in my mind I played out my meeting with her. At midnight, I threw back the covers and sank myself into my novel, thankful for something with the power to distract me. Sometime in the night I woke up at the keyboard and stumbled into bed. I woke at seven without a prayer of getting back to sleep even though I was tired. Illyssa sensed my shifting about in bed and got up, too. She made breakfast. I couldn't eat.

"Are you going to come with me?" I asked.

"I don't know if I should," she said. "Maybe I'll come, but wait outside. I think you should see her alone first, don't you?"

"I guess I should," I said. "But you come and wait."

"I will."

Illyssa went to her shop. I spent the morning taking a shower and changing my clothes a dozen times. I wanted to make the right impression. I was scared and I was excited. I was more nervous than I'd been before any sporting event, even the state wrestling championships when I had to go out under the spotlight by myself in front of thousands of people and face the defending AAU national champion for the state title. After I won that match, I promptly staggered to the side of the mat and vomited into a bucket. Now I was thankful to have nothing in my stomach.

I picked Illyssa up in front of her store. She would wait in the truck outside The Varsity, a cafeteria-style restaurant near the university.

"What do I say?" I said.

"You'll know what to say," Illyssa told me. "Just talk to her."

I kissed her and got out of the truck.

"Good luck," she told me through the open window.

"Thanks," I said. I was in a total fog.

I walked into The Varsity, scared to death, floating like I was on drugs. I saw her right away and meandered through a long row of tables and chairs until I could slide into the booth against the wall.

"Hi," I said across the table, without reaching for her.

"Hello, I'm Martha," she said quietly, her lip trembling slightly.

Martha, I thought, what a nice name. She was younger than I thought she'd look. The only thing that suggested any age at all were a few strands of gray that highlighted her long frizzy dark hair. She was thin and nervous and appeared very normal except for two prominent circles of blush on her cheeks that were too red for her pale skin and somehow mixed very incongruously with her wide-brimmed straw hat. Her eyes were dull gray and shifted quickly about my face, assessing me. In those eyes I saw nothing I could recognize of myself. It was obvious to me at that moment that I had made much more in my mind of the innate connection between a biological mother and son than was real.

"You're my son," she said, a smile passing across her face then quickly disappearing.

"I didn't even know you existed until recently," she said somberly. "I wasn't well. There was something in my past that I had repressed. It was you. I knew I was ill, most of my life. I just didn't know why. Then, two years ago, in therapy . . . I found out. . . . "

Her face crinkled with pain, leaving her to look like a pathetic broken clown. I knew then from my college education, as I know now from the facts of my life, that it is certainly possible, even common, for a person to experience events so traumatic that they will be submerged into the subconscious regions of their mind.

"When I was eleven . . ." she choked, "I was raped . . . by my father."

I felt the whole place spinning around me, swimming in little spots of light. How could I be that? How could everything I had achieved and everything I had become be the product of a heinous crime? This then was the fissure like flaw in me. It was a chasm. That black yawning pit of hell in my nightmares was really the source of who I was, the spawn of an act vomited from those evil depths. My father was my grandfather, a pedophile with a soul so diseased with rot that he could rape his own daughter. It was unspeakable. It still is.

"But," I heard myself saying through the spinning blur, "it said you were in college. It said my father was in the army. . . . "

"Everything was falsified," she explained desperately. "My parents were involved with social services. They were foster parents for many of the children who went through services. They knew everyone. Everything was fabricated. You were taken from me and it was as if the whole thing never happened, a cover-up. . . . "

"I don't know," I said.

"You're my son," she told me painfully. She reached across the table then and grasped my hand. Her touch was cold and bony, but desperately firm.

"I know you are," she said.

"I . . . I have to think," I said, pulling away. "I have to go."

I staggered up and backed away from her pain-twisted face as if she were a monster. She wasn't a monster. She was a woman victimized by one. But I couldn't see that then. I could only feel my own terror as everything inside me began to fall apart. The elaborate sand castles of my identity melted into the roiling salt water of her news, leaving me with nothing but a pile of disgusting glop.

The conversation was like a dream to me. I listened to her story with the feeling of a man grasping a ledge, hanging tenuously from the parapet of a skyscraper, where the thrill of the height and the rushing howl of the wind block out all other sensations. Out on the sidewalk, one by one I recounted her words. They hammered my fingers, separating them, and me, from the grip I had on the life I had always known. I lost my hold on reality and on everything I'd always believed about who I was. I spun in a downward free fall, relishing the thought of the earth's terrible kiss that would send me mercifully into unknowing darkness.

Tears raced down my cheeks and my own face twisted in mental agony. I was appalled with myself. I was ashamed. I was horrified at who I was. For three years I had fantasized about how I had come to be the person so many people admired and celebrated. In my pride I assumed my parents could only have been exceptional. I had so foolishly envisioned my mother to be a tragic figure of noble lineage and my father to be a gallant gentleman, unable to stay together or keep me because of cruel Shakespearean circumstances beyond either of their control. Instead, I was born of an insanity and a violence too horrible to be considered. How could the rot of my conception not have infiltrated me? It was impossible. That meant that I had somehow fooled everyone. It meant that at the core, I was rotten, too.

"Oh, my God," I said. I was at the truck, sitting beside Illyssa. I let my head fall slowly across the seat toward her shoulder.

"Tim," she said, putting her arms around me. "What happened. What did she say?"

Sobs shook my frame.

"My God! Oh, my God," I moaned, "I had to know. I had to know. Oh, my God . . . "

"Tim, what is it? What did she say?"

I don't know how I told her, and I don't know how long it took me to tell it. Time seemed to have no measure. But Illyssa held me. She listened, and I waited for the horror and revulsion to creep onto her face. It never did.

Instead, she pursed her lips and said, "That's not your mother."

She said it with defiance and authority.

"How can you say that?" I said incredulously.

"Because she's not. Tim, look at me. I know. She's not your mother. That's not your mother. There's no way that could be you."

"How can you say that?"

In a way, her adamant refusal to accept the situation made it that much more difficult to bear because it confirmed my fears that it was too horrible for even Illyssa to accept. If I was in fact that woman's son, it meant I was a freak so detestable that I was beyond love. I was beyond marriage, beyond parenthood, a seed that must not be allowed to propagate.

"You know I know these kinds of things," she told me, playing the trump card she normally chose to hold.

I knew that, but how could I hope?

"That can't be your mother. I know it, Tim."

She kept assuring me. She kept holding me.

"How can I know? How can I find out?" I said.

"We'll go to the agency," she told me. "You'll tell them what's happened. They'll have to tell you. They'll have to at least tell you if she's *not* your mother."

"But she said everything was forged," I pointed out.

"You have to go, Tim."

Neither of us remembered Evelyn's name, but I remembered where the yellow brick building was, just off Salina Street, one of the main thoroughfares of the city.

"I need to speak to the director," I told the receptionist.

"Evelyn?" she said quizzically.

"Yes, Evelyn. My name is Tim Green," I told her. "I'm the football player from SU. I've spoken to her before. She knows me."

The receptionist nodded and got up from her desk. Illyssa held my hand as we stood there waiting. I wondered if she would ever hold it again. I was certain that if Illyssa were wrong I would lose her. If she was wrong and I was the son of a monster, laden with incestuous genes, she could never be my wife. I knew she, like me, wanted a family. Children would be impossible with the likes of me.

The receptionist returned and solemnly led us to Evelyn's austere office. She stood to greet us and was obviously surprised to hear from me after so long.

"I know you can't tell me who my mother is," I said to her without sitting down and without preamble, "but I've just met a woman, her name is Martha. She's telling me she's my mother. You have to tell me if she is. . . . "

I didn't give Evelyn a chance to argue. I launched into Martha's story.

"Is this my mother?" I demanded when I'd finished.

Evelyn hesitated, then sat down and cleared her throat.

"No," she said, obviously uncomfortable disclosing even the slightest bit of information. "I know the woman you're talking about, Martha. She's been here to see me before. She's not your mother."

Illyssa squeezed my hand.

"How do you know?" I demanded. "How can you say that?" I felt a wave of relief, but I was wary not to allow myself too much comfort. Anyone can be fooled by a good fraud.

"She said the records were fabricated," I told her. "How can you know?"

"I know, because the woman who handled your case remembered your mother," Evelyn said.

"She remembered her?" I said, bewildered. "How?"

"It's unusual," Evelyn admitted. "Of course, every caseworker handles hundreds of adoptions through the years, but there was a woman here for many years, Mrs. Bruckner, who remembered your mother. When you called and came in the first time, she told me about your mother. Mrs. Bruckner said your mother came back after you were born. She was adamant that you be adopted by parents who both had college educations. Mrs. Bruckner said your mother came back a year after you were born to make sure that the agency had done what she'd requested.

"She remembered your mother, because, in all the years she worked for the agency, she'd never seen a woman come back. Your mother was the only one. So I know this woman, Martha, is not your mother. You don't have to worry. . . .

"And," she continued, "I'm familiar with Martha. She's come here before as well, demanding that we help her find the son she thinks she's lost. She's a disturbed woman."

"Is it true?" I asked. "What she's saying happened to her?"

Evelyn considered this, then said, "I don't know. There's no way to know. She's very ill."

"Yes," I said, "of course."

"Can I speak to Mrs. Bruckner?" I asked.

"She's no longer here," Evelyn said. "She recently retired."

"Can you tell me where she is?" I begged. "I need to talk with her."

"I can't say," Evelyn told me. "I think she moved to Houston. Her daughter lives there. That's all I can tell you. Her name is Annette, Annette Bruckner."

"Thank you, Evelyn. Thank you very much."

"Good luck," she said with a sad smile. "I'm sorry I can't help you any more. I've probably already said more than I should."

Twenty-three

I called directory information in the Houston area and found Annette Bruckner. She was kind, but either could not or chose not to recall anything specific about my mother. I implored her to help me, but she was adamant. She admitted remembering my mother, but only as a nebulous figure whose deeds, rather than identification, had stuck in her mind. Remembering the advice in the ALMA material, I left Mrs. Bruckner my name and phone number, asking if she would please call me should some bit of information spring into her mind at some later date. I was back almost to where I'd started, eliminating only one tragic set of circumstances from the endless possible histories that resulted in my birth.

That night we had dinner with Stu and Colleen. We were at a small family-style Italian place called Angotti's when I recounted what had happened with Martha to Stu and Colleen.

He shook his head and said, "Uh-oh. I told you. I told you not to do this."

"It turned out all right, Stu," I reminded him. "That's not my mother."

"No, that's not," he said, "but why do you want to keep looking? You were lucky this time. But you don't need to do this to yourself. Why would you keep going?"

I looked to Illyssa and said, "Don't you think I have to find her?"

She nodded slowly and said, "He does, Stu. He needs to find out. It bothers him."

"He's done pretty well without knowing up 'til now," Stu said, taking an angry sip of his Snapple soda through a straw.

"Did you know about the dream he had a couple of weeks ago?" she asked him. "Did he tell you?"

"No," Stu said, "what dream?"

Illyssa looked at me and I nodded, then looked down at my plate.

"He has dreams, nightmares . . ." she said. "The other night, he woke up and was running around the house with a loaded shotgun. He was asleep. He was going on about how they were coming for him."

"My God," Stu said.

"I've had the dreams my whole life," I said, looking up at my friend. "I can't get out of them. I'm awake, but I'm still in the dream. I can't get out."

"Until I get him in the shower or get him to eat something," Illyssa said. "I think he has to do something physical to get him out of it."

"If I go back to sleep," I explained, "the dream just keeps going."

"He can't get out," Illyssa said.

"I don't get them like I used to," I told them, squeezing Illyssa's hand. "Not since Illyssa."

"He needs to find out," she repeated to Colleen.

A few nights later, Illyssa and I were having dinner at The Retreat, a local bar and restaurant in the heart of the village of Liverpool, planning the best way to proceed.

"You have to go back to the beginning and go through everything again," Illyssa told me.

"Meaning what?"

"I mean, sometimes when you're looking for something, it's in the most obvious place," she told me. "Remember last week, you were looking everywhere for your pen?"

"And it was in my mouth. . . . "

She smiled warmly, trying to keep a lid on her quiet laugh.

"We all do it," she said. "Sometimes the thing you're looking for is right there . . . sometimes it's not."

"But why not try, right?" I said wearily, wondering where exactly I'd start over from.

We paid the bill and walked out into the cold evening. The winter's snow was gone, but the village of Liverpool sits at the edge of Onondaga Lake, and a bitter wind whipped through the streets of the village, swaying the power lines overhead. We pulled our coats close and locked arms, walking briskly toward the car in the dim yellow light of the streetlamps that illuminated the sidewalk. When we rounded the corner, I pulled Illyssa to me and switched sides with her. Coming toward us in the darkness was a disheveled figure with long hair and not nearly enough clothes on to fend off the cold. My back stiffened and the hair sprang up on the back of my neck, primal instincts preparing for trouble.

"Kyle," I said reflexively and relaxed. I had recognized his gait before I could even make out his face. It was my brother.

"Hey, man," he said in his gruff casual manner, as if he'd seen me that morning at breakfast.

"Where've you been?" I asked, amazed at his sudden appearance.

"Around."

He gave us a brief recount of the past year. After he left D.C., Kyle went on a dark odyssey across the Northeast, traveling by bus from city to city, living off the money he'd made until that ran out, then going to another city and another menial job until finally ending up on the street. He lived day to day, meal to meal, never knowing where he was going to go next or why. The confusion I felt within myself, the doubts about who I was, Kyle was living out in his life.

This was the worst shape I'd ever seen him in. He was thinner than I could ever remember, and he grasped at his own arms to fend off the cold. His hair was so long and wild that it was nearly impossible to make out his face. Life had beaten him down. He couldn't look at me or anyone else. He directed his words, like his gaze, at the ground.

We took him home to our duplex and fed him a couple of tuna sandwiches. He ate as if it was his first meal in days, and he drank almost a gallon of milk. I offered him a bed, but he refused. The only way I could convince him to stay was by letting him sleep on the floor in the living room underneath the worn blanket that lay across the back of our couch. He would allow himself nothing more than that.

I had known, probably within the first few hours of knowing her, that Illyssa was the woman I wanted to spend the rest of my life with. We knew from the past year that the practical aspects of living together presented no obstacles to the genuine love and respect that we shared. Marriage was the next natural step. I wanted to surprise her though, so one weekend in May, when we were up at a summer house we had on Raquette Lake in the Adirondack Mountains, I asked Illyssa to go for a boat ride, just the two of us, before dinner. We had guests, and she was putting together some dinner in the kitchen with a couple of her friends, but after a little pestering, she agreed.

The sun was setting in the west amid a parade of orange sky, purple clouds, and forest-green mountains. In the east, a perfect yellow crescent moon had already risen. I stopped the boat in the middle of the lake amid this splendor and took a bottle of Dom Perignon out of the cooler resting on the floor of the boat.

"What's this?" she asked.

"I want to propose a toast," I said, opening the bottle and pouring two glasses of champagne. Before I gave Illyssa her glass, I dropped a diamond ring, suspended in a cube of ice, into her drink so it would float in the middle of the glass.

"To us," I said, trying not to choke on my words or spill my upraised glass, which shook uncontrollably in my unsteady hand. "Hopefully forever. Will you marry me?"

"Tim," she said, beginning to cry, "I had no idea. I can't believe you did this. . . . "

"I love you," I said.

"I love you so much."

"Will you? Will you marry me?"

"Of course I'll marry you," she said. The tears ran down her cheeks on either side of her broad smile. "I can't believe you did this."

I kissed her then, and we drank our champagne, rocking gently in the soft dark water under the setting sun and the rising moon. I took the ring out of her glass and broke the ice around it with my teeth.

"Put it on," I said proudly. "I can't believe you're going to be my wife."

"You knew I would," she said.

"I know," I said. "You make me so happy."

"You make me happy. You've made me happy."

I said I knew, but I didn't know. It seemed so perfect for us to be together, to get married, to have a family the way each of us had always said we wanted to. I knew if Illyssa said yes on that boat that we would be together forever. I knew she was my Penelope from *The Odyssey*, my Mercedes from *The Count of Monte Cristo*. Unlike any woman I had loved before, I knew that if she said she'd never leave me, she never would. It was the most fulfilling moment of my life, and after that, the bad dreams nearly disappeared.

Twenty-four

Despite the excitement of the wedding we were planning for the following year, rehabilitating my brother occupied much of those spring and summer months. Illyssa's patience and caring finally got Kyle to the point where he could look at people again, although not directly in the eye. She convinced him to cut his hair, and I helped him get another job. He accompanied us often to dinners, movies, and get-togethers with our friends. Everyone treated Kyle like he belonged, and it allowed the kind and engaging person beneath the battered exterior to emerge.

He began to think beyond where he would get his next meal and how he might pay for a new pair of sneakers. He stayed off drugs, even though he'd drink a little too much from time to time. (I probably didn't help him there.) And he began to dream a little bit about what he might do in the future.

He settled on being a truck driver. He liked the open road, the freedom, the hours, and he just liked to drive. There was a tractor trailer driving school not far from our place, and I took him there to enroll. The program would take about three months. That meant that Kyle would have to finish it up after Illyssa and I had already left for Atlanta. I was a little uneasy about leaving the place to Kyle on his own, but I saw big things for my brother in the truck-driving business. I suppose I'd been captivated by the slogan of the school that I'd seen on a raised red-and-blue plastic sign that hung above the receptionist's window: "Trucking: It's More Than a Job, It's a Way of Life."

It was easy for me to envision my brother hauling big rigs coast to coast with loads of soap or livestock or dangerous chemicals. He could wear his cowboy hats without drawing so much as a second look. He could smoke his cigarettes, drink his whiskey, and prowl for women at roadhouses like some character from a hard-boiled detective novel. It was a romantic image I had created for Kyle, even if it was a little rough. He seemed captivated by it as well.

I was in the midst of helping Kyle get things organized when Illyssa announced that she'd gotten a call from the mother of my young friend Timmy Dumbrowski, the boy I'd kept in touch with.

"They invited us for a cookout," Illyssa told me. "We should go, you know. It would mean a lot to them."

We both knew that times were hard for more people than just Kyle. Sally Dumbrowski, Tim's mom, had told Illyssa she was afraid she was losing control of her kids. With no husband and a demanding job, it seemed to her with each passing day that they grew farther apart. Tim and his two brothers were going wild. It was a worthy cause, but I was wrapped up in getting my brother off the ground, and with everything else going on, I wasn't keen on throwing myself into another set of people's problems. Nevertheless, Illyssa's more generous nature won out and she set a date for us to drive up to the Dumbrowskis', where I would act as a surrogate uncle and try to whip the young boys into line, or at least get them to give their mom a little more respect.

During that time, on a surreptitious trip to my parents' house to get some things for Kyle that he'd left in his bedroom, I remembered Illyssa's advice about starting back from the beginning in the search for my mother. Since I was there for Kyle, sneaking around my childhood home like a thief anyway, I decided it wouldn't be a bad idea to take a look at my parents' papers again. This time I knew right where they were and exactly what I was looking for.

I glanced over the medical report that I had already copied. I poked at the newspaper article about my adoption, recognizing now the name of Annette Bruckner as an important player in the drama. I looked carefully at this article for something I might have missed before. There was nothing I could see. I went through other papers my parents had: insurance policies, mortgage notes, and even copies of their wills, although I didn't read them. Finally, I came to my original birth certificate. It was printed and stamped on thick-gauge, light-green paper. The state seal had been pressed into the document twenty-four years ago. I scrutinized this document. I'd seen it before. It had been required through the years to prove my age when I did things like get my paper route or obtain my driver's license.

It was then that I noticed something that had escaped my attention before. Not only did the certificate list the state in which I was born—New York—it named the town as well—Oswego. This was an entirely new angle. Heretofore, I had scattered my attentions between the four hospitals in the Syracuse area. I wasn't even born in Syracuse. I never sought someone within any of the four hospitals to search the medical records for me, because I hadn't known which one I was born in. The prospect of finding four different people willing to clandestinely search sealed medical records had been too daunting.

But, there was only one hospital, that I knew of, in Oswego. With the Oswego Hospital as my specific target, I felt encouraged that I could somehow find someone on the inside who would be willing to accept money for the information I was seeking. I'd never been involved with bribes or graft or payoffs before, but I'd read enough books to know that those kinds of things went on all the time. The trick would be to find someone who was willing, without alerting hospital authorities. Contacting the wrong person from the start could prove disastrous. It was quite a dilemma for an artless kid from Liverpool.

The whole way home I imagined myself meeting people in back rooms or the corner booth of dark restaurants late at night, arranging the deal and making the proper payoffs. It could be done, of that I had no doubt. I had the medical information from my birth. If I could get someone who could access the records for the day I was born, all they would have to do would be to cross-reference my information with all the male babies born that day. When they found a match, they could also find the corresponding information on my mother: her name, address, and possibly even more.

When I brought the question of how to Illyssa, she reminded me that a good friend of mine, Ike Morrison, was a doctor. Ike could at least give me some insight into the parameters I would be working within. When I got him on the phone, he was skeptical.

"Somebody could lose everything they had if they got caught," he told me. "Probably a doctor or a nurse could do it, but they'd not only lose their job, they might lose their license for something like that. I can't imagine anyone doing it for you. It's dangerous. . . . "

This was nothing I didn't already know.

"There's something else," he told me.

"What?"

"You're running out of time."

"What do you mean?" I asked.

"I mean that most hospitals don't save their records after twenty-five years. That's all they're required to save them by law," he said. "You don't have much time, do you?"

"I turn twenty-five this coming December," I told him.

"You've got a couple of months," he said. "Whatever you do, you've got to do it quick. Once those records are discarded . . . you won't ever get another crack at them."

"Tim," Illyssa said when I'd hung up the phone, "you said Oswego Hospital."

"Yeah," I replied. "That's the only hospital in the town of Oswego, and the birth certificate said that was the town I was born in. It had to be there."

"Sally Dumbrowski," Illyssa said, directing a steady gaze into my eyes.

I felt my heart pump faster.

"Huh," I said, "of course. Oh, man," I said shaking my head, "how can I ask her?"

Illyssa took my elbows into her hands and made me look into her eyes.

"You have to ask her," she told me. "This is probably going to be your only chance. This was meant to be. You didn't do what you've done for her or Timmy because of this," she reminded me. "You didn't even know you were going to look for your mother when you first met them. You did it to be nice, and now she can help you."

"But her job . . ."

"It will be all right," Illyssa told me with that certain look on her face. "She'll be fine. She'll do this for you, Tim. You've helped her. She'll help you. We're going there on Tuesday night. I don't want you to have to go through the rest of your life torturing yourself because you don't know."

Her words reminded me of all the times I had awakened her in the middle of the night over the past few years tossing fitfully, grinding my teeth in terror.

"I'm alone," I had said to her so many times in the midst of my delirium. "I'm completely alone. I don't know where I'm going, and I don't know where I've come from. I'm afraid I'm never going to find her."

"This is your chance," Illyssa told me now. "You ask her. You have to."

Twenty-five

A milky white blanket of clouds in the west fended off the brunt of a hot evening sun. Sally Dumbrowski lived with her three boys about forty minutes north of Syracuse, just off the highway. The old yellow house stood straight and narrow, and the boys were throwing a ball around in a wide green backyard when we pulled into the gravel drive. Instead of rushing to the car to greet us or feign indifference, the kids just stopped what they were doing and stared, shifting uncomfortably from one foot to the other.

"Hey, guys," I said, brandishing some Falcon stuff I'd brought for them.

"Wow," moaned the littlest one as I handed him a T-shirt.

"Will you sign it?" Timmy asked.

"For five bucks," I told him.

His face froze.

"Kidding," I said, and all three of them beamed.

Sally came off the front porch, a heavy plate of cellophane-covered burgers in one hand and a long-handled spatula in the other.

"Hello," she said, blushing at the sight of the booty in the hands of her three thugs. "You didn't have to do that."

"No problem," I said with an offhand wave that I hoped masked the guilt that I presumed stood out on my face like a raspberry rash.

"Well," she said, "we're really glad you could come. . . . I'm going to put the meat on and we can eat. Would you like to sit down? I've got some lemonade."

We sat at the picnic table on the lawn. It was all laid out with a red-checkered tablecloth and what I presumed were Sally's best plates and utensils. The kids hovered about me, asking questions.

"Did you ever sack Joe Montana?"

"Yup."

"No . . . for real?"

"Got him for real."

"How about Elway?"

"Not yet, but we haven't played Denver, so you can't hold it against me."

"Does it hurt? To play, I mean."

"Yeah, it hurts. You get hurt just about every game."

"But you keep playing?"

"Yeah. You have to."

"Cool."

No detail was too small for me to reveal, but it did me good to go over them and remember the enthusiasm that young boys have for the NFL. I became aware of the fact that I had misplaced some of that joy in the grinding daily life of working, sweating, bleeding, and most times losing despite it all, since I played for the Atlanta Falcons. Losing didn't mean anything to these kids, though. I was like a circus act, a real live NFL player. I had taken Joe Montana to the turf, actually had my hands on him. They reached out surreptitiously as we spoke and touched my arms.

We ate, and the kids eyed me over the tops of their burgers, marveling at the amounts I could consume. Sally beamed with nervous delight. Not only were her three ruffians happy, they actually showed some manners.

After homemade rhubarb pie and ice cream, the kids were ready for some action.

"Let him sit, boys," Sally told them.

"You guys start a game, I'll be with you in a few minutes," I told them. "Let me talk to your mom."

"They listen to you a lot better than they do to me," she said under her breath. One eye was on her boys as they bounced around the yard like pinballs.

I shrugged, not knowing what to say. Illyssa was giving me a look that said the time was right.

"Sally, I want to ask you a favor."

She gave me a puzzled, embarrassed look, as if there was no favor too large for her to grant.

"I don't want you to feel like you have to do this," I explained. "I'll understand completely if you can't."

She gave me a nervous little laugh and dug absently at her pie with a silver fork.

"I want you to know that this is something I didn't know about until just recently. Meeting you, and Timmy, and staying in touch with him over the years . . . "

"All right," she said patiently. Her round cheeks were flushed from the cooking and the heat. She brushed back a curly strand of her yellow hair.

"So I don't know if you even know this, but I was adopted when I was an infant. I've been looking for my biological mother now for about four years. The records are sealed with the state, and everything I've tried hasn't worked. A couple of days ago, I found out from an original birth certificate that I was born at Oswego—"

A yelp went up from the yard. Someone had scored.

"I have a medical record from the day I was born," I told her. "It's got my height and weight and some other things on it. Of course, my mother's name isn't on it. But I was thinking that if someone, if you . . . could match my record to the baby boys born that day at the hospital, that you could get the original record. I think it would have my mother's name on it, maybe even her address. . . .

"I understand what I'm asking," I told her, looking out over the yard, not wanting to intimidate her with my stare. "I don't want you to feel like you have to say yes. But I had to ask. I don't know what else to do. The records will probably be, I don't know, thrown out or destroyed in December. It'll be twenty-five years—"

"Of course I'll do it," she said with certainty.

I looked up. She wore a small satisfied smile on her round red face.

"You don't have to," I said once more.

"I know that," she said. "I want to. I think I know how I can do it, too. I conduct studies from time to time anyway, to gauge our effectiveness as compared to the hospital in the past. I can just choose babies born in December 1963 as my control group. It shouldn't be that hard. I'm glad you came to me now, though. It will take some time to get this going, and I'll have to get approval. I should be able to make it by December, but it will probably be close. Administration at the hospital is pretty much like everywhere else, it moves slow."

It was as simple as it was perfect. It was hard for me then, as it is to this day, not to believe that, as Illyssa had said, the whole thing was meant to be.

Twenty-six

When it was time to leave again for Atlanta, I was faced with the decision of what to do with Kyle. He was halfway through his truck driver's training course, bright with the prospect of having a marketable skill. Job placement for graduates was running at about 90 percent. Kyle assured me that since he was the best driver in his class, it would be a slam dunk for him to get a job and be on his way to financial independence. As it was, he had been living with Illyssa and me. Our two-bedroom town house seemed to be getting smaller by the day. Kyle is a wonderful guy, but he lives by his own peculiar set of rules that don't always coincide with everyone else's.

Against my better judgment, I left him a set of keys for the house. At least, I pointed out to Illyssa, I put my foot down when he asked me to leave my truck behind. Instead, I bought him a bike so he could ride the two miles to the truck school. If he wanted to drive trucks that badly, I reasoned with him, he could bike it for a few weeks. He didn't see the logic in that, but I knew him well enough not to mistake his annoyance for ingratitude. With strict instructions not to disrupt the neighborhood, we left Kyle for the Atlanta Falcons.

My third NFL season began abominably. Two days before the opening game, in the final drill of the day, my arm got caught between two players, inverting my elbow, tearing the ligaments, and blotting me out of the starting lineup for five weeks. When I returned, however, things started to finally go right. I got back into the starting lineup and began to excel on the NFL field the way I had in college. In November, I received a copy of my mother's medical record from Sally Dumbrowski in the mail. When I called Sally to thank her, she told me that a week after she'd made the original copy, she'd gone back to see if there was anything more in the file that she'd overlooked.

"I was nervous the first time," she explained. "I just grabbed the first page of the record and ran out of there. I copied it and put it back, but then got to thinking that there might be more.

"When I went back a few days ago," she told me, "they were gone. If you can believe it, there was a fire in that storage room and everything was destroyed. I can't believe I got it. If I'd been one week later, you never would have known."

My mother was Joanne Burgen. Her husband, and the man listed as my father, was Edward Burgen. I knew whoever Edward was that he must have been the man who married my mother in the eighth month of her pregnancy, not my real father. There was also an address on the medical form: 116 Putman Street, Syracuse, New York. I looked over this document countless times, absorbing my mother's name and every other bit of the limited information it contained.

It was time for another private detective. With my new information, someone had to be able to track her down. I went to see Al Miller, the NFL security agent for the Atlanta Falcons, for some advice. Each NFL team has a security agent. Most of them are retired from the FBI. Al was a grandfatherly man who always wore tweed jackets. He was pleasant and gentle with a short gray haircut and black plastic glasses. I wanted the name of a good detective in the upstate New York area who could help me find Joanne, maybe an old FBI agent. I'd gone sour on Doyle.

I ended up explaining everything to Al, and he, like everyone who's ever heard the story, was fascinated.

"You know," he told me, enthusiastic at the notion of coaching me through the machinations of being a detective, "a lot of this work you could do yourself. I'll ask around and see if I can't find someone to help, but every city has directories that list people not only by their names but by their addresses. Sometimes they list the companies people work for. You could probably find the directory from 1963 in the Syracuse library and see what information you could find. You never know.

"Also," he added, "you might want to go to the house and see who lives there now. Talk to some of the neighbors. It was twenty-five years ago, but you never know. Some neighbor may have had Christmas dinner with your mother back then and for some reason remembers it even now. Especially up in that area, where people know who you are. They're a lot more likely to help. You're a lot better off doing it yourself than having a detective asking around."

I thanked Al for his suggestions, but still asked him to help me find a private detective. The season would be over in a few weeks, and I'd be back home. I was supposed to start law school at the university, and my novel was in full swing. The prospect of turning myself into a detective along with everything else wasn't thrilling. I'd do some of it, no doubt, but I wanted a professional on the case as well.

"You know," he said pensively, "the guy for the New York Jets is an old friend of mine. His name is Melvin Rowe. He used to be with the Albany DA's office. I'll ask him if he knows anyone. He might be able to run a DMV for you too, in case your mother is still in the state somewhere."

"With the same name," I reminded him.

"Yes," he said, "that's true. A woman married to a man under those circumstances isn't all that likely to still be married to him twenty-five years later. She could have an entirely new name. . . . "

"And he could be anywhere," I said.

"So could she," he replied. "Even though you have a name, I hate to tell you, it might not be that much at all. . . . Well, I'll try my contacts and find someone for you. You try what I told you when you get back home. I think your best bet may be with the neighbors. Keep in touch."

Kyle graduated from his truck-driving school and passed his class-one road test. He was a real truck driver, and ready for a new way of life.

However, the people in the placement office at his school seemed not to see things quite the same way as Kyle. He felt they were cheating him by not getting him a job with one of the better truck companies out on the road.

"It's a scam," he informed me authoritatively over the phone one night. "I can outdrive anyone at this school, including the instructors. . . . I can back a rig between two barrels without hardly looking in my mirrors. I can downshift from sixteen to four as quick as you can count. I can skip gears even. Hell, they want me to work for some damn company that doesn't even pay you overtime. That's bullshit!"

"Kyle," I reasoned patiently, "can't you just take whatever job they get you? Just for starters? Who cares if it's not exactly what you want? Just get out there and get some experience, then look for a place that has everything you want."

Our minds were obviously not of the same mettle, and Kyle, determined to do things his way, told me to forget the whole thing. Two weeks later, he called me, completely dejected. He'd wasted his time chasing a dream that wasn't going to come true. He was hanging up the idea of big rigs out on the open road.

"Kyle," I pleaded, "you can't just quit. Go back to the school and see if they can get you one of those jobs."

"Can't," he told me.

"Why not?"

"I told the head guy to go fuck himself. They were all full of shit anyway."

I moaned in exasperation, but my mind was already beginning to work.

"Come down here," I told him.

"To Atlanta?"

"Yes," I said, "there are driving jobs everywhere down here. I can help you out. I'll find something for you down here."

"You think so?"

I could tell already that he liked the idea of coming to Atlanta. The tone of his voice was beginning to brighten.

"Yeah," I said, wondering if my enthusiasm had outrun my sense, "but you've got to take a job if I get it for you."

"Oh, I will," he assured me.

"Any job driving," I warned.

"You think you can really get something in Atlanta? I'm a Southerner deep down anyway."

"I'll get something."

"How will I get down there?"

I sent him money for a bus ticket, and four days later, Kyle moved into our golf course condo. Within two weeks, he was out on the road hauling paper products all across the United States. He found himself a girlfriend and moved in with her. The road seemed to be the perfect place for Kyle. While he was discovering what looked to be his future, I was intent on my past.

Twenty-seven

About the time Kyle came to Atlanta, I heard through my parents that my old Little League coach, Ron Kelly, was very sick. He'd moved to North Carolina years before, and we had lost touch with him. Through some mutual friends, my parents learned that he was suffering from brain cancer.

"I thought you should know," my father said over the phone. He also gave me my old coach's number.

When I called Coach Kelly, he was thrilled. He told me all about how he was going through chemotherapy, radiation, and surgery in order to beat his disease.

"I'll get it, Timmy," he told me, unable to think of me as anything but the young kid I had been.

I invited Ron to see a Falcons game. He wasn't an Atlanta fan; he lived and died for the New York Giants. I told him we were playing the Giants in three weeks, and he made plans to come down with his son.

That day I sacked Phil Simms, but the Giants came back in the last seconds to win the game. Coach Kelly told me afterward that it was the perfect day for him. I had played well and gotten to the quarterback just the way he'd taught me as an eight-year-old. Meantime, the Giants had won.

"I'm sorry, Timmy," he explained. We were standing outside the stadium in the player's parking lot. His shaved and scarred head drew stares. "But I just had to root for the Giants."

"I'm glad you saw the game," I told him. "It's no Rose Bowl, but I guess it's close."

"It's better than the Rose Bowl," he told me, hugging me and reaching up to tousle my hair.

That was the last time I saw him.

I saw Al Miller several times before the season ended, but he hadn't heard back from any of his FBI contacts and couldn't give me the name of anyone to help. The prospect of conducting my own investigation looked imminent. I refused to just call any private detective out of the Yellow Pages. I had no idea what I'd get.

The first week we got back to Syracuse, Illyssa and I spent time catching up with friends we hadn't seen in six months. My parents and I found various reasons as to why we couldn't arrive at a mutually acceptable date to get together, but uncomfortably promised we'd find time soon. Then Illyssa and I took a week's vacation in the Caribbean before law school began. When we returned, I gave Al Miller a couple of calls, but kept missing him. I registered for my classes, got my books, and began the grind of a first-year law student.

Within two weeks I had settled into the daily routine of classes, workouts, time with Illyssa, reading my law books, and writing my novel late into the night. There wasn't much time for sleep, but busy as I was, my annoyance with Al Miller kept spilling into my conscious thoughts on a regular basis. Finally, I got hold of him. He'd been working harder for me than I thought.

"Sorry I haven't gotten back to you," he apologized. "I got in touch with Melvin Rowe from the Jets, and he was going to run the DMV for me. I wanted to wait to call you until I had some news from him. I thought I might be able to tell you that I found her . . . but I didn't. There is no Joanne Burgen with a driver's license in the state of New York. In fact, there never was. Melvin went all the way back to 1963, that's why it took so long. He had to have somebody in Albany look it up in a file. There was no record. I'm sorry."

"Well," I said, not feeling too bad since I hadn't expected it to happen that easily anyway, "that's all right. I appreciate your trying. What about a detective?"

"The closest guy I can find who comes really highly recommended is in Rochester," he told me. "So it's going to cost a lot of money for you to have him drive in to research the stuff I told you about in the Syracuse library. That's all he's going to do, I'm telling you. I'll give you his name, but I still think you should just run this down yourself."

I thanked Al again for all he'd done and took the name. I called the detective right away. He was less than thrilled with the assignment I had for him and asked why I didn't want to just look up the information myself. I figured the detective business must have been pretty good in Rochester for the guy to be asking me such a question and finally figured I would be better off doing it myself. I don't know why I had resisted it so much in the first place.

I was busy at the time, but I think it was more than that. I think that in a way I felt I now had a thin thread that connected me directly to my mother. I had her name. If I stressed that connection too hard by looking, it might break and be gone. This was my last hope, and I think I was almost happier with the hope than I was with the prospect of spoiling it.

Nevertheless, I began to search myself. The next day, I got a map and found Putman Street. Illyssa went with me on a drive to the west side of Syracuse. It was an unusually mild day for that time of year. We exited the highway and passed through a maze of car dealerships and electronics stores. Every corner was capped with a heap of dirty snow. The roads quickly began to deteriorate and people of all colors spilled out onto the steps of abandoned storefronts.

The fact that I was born of this poverty became undeniable; 116 Putman Street was just this side of being condemned. Where the exterior walls weren't patched with cheap raw particle board, a faded, creamy orange paint showed through the grime. There was a man with bad teeth in a heavy wool coat sitting on the decrepit front porch. He remained in his seat, a worn-out La-Z-Boy, but two young kids tumbled out of the house as we pulled into the broken driveway. The kids, one boy and one girl, only went as far as the steps before a bark from the man held them at bay.

A quick glance up and down the street told me why my new red truck had piqued their interest. Mine was the only vehicle undamaged by a recent accident or unblemished by terminal rust.

Illyssa waited in the front seat. I got out, but stopped just short of the steps.

"Hello," I said to the man, "I'm Tim Green . . . "

I could see some glimmer of recognition in his pale but thickly stubbled face.

"I used to play football at SU," I told him.

"You are, aren't you?" he said, shifting his massive bulk in the chair to get a better look.

"Yes," I said, smiling big at him and then again down at the kids. "I'm looking for someone who used to live here. Have you been in this house long?"

His doleful, weepy eyes were jaundiced and bloodshot. "I rent this place," he grumbled. "Had it about four years now."

"Oh. Could you tell me who owns it?"

"Name by Coates, Mildred Coates. She's the landlord. . . . "

I nodded and asked, "Could you tell me how to get in touch with her? Do you have her phone number?"

"It'd be in the house," he said, obviously trying to decide whether or not it was worth the effort for him to get out of the chair. "Would you sign some autographs for the kids?"

"I'd be happy to."

That put him over the edge, and he worked his way up out of the chair. The porch complained under his weight and the door screeched loudly when he opened it. The kids looked awestruck, not because I was someone they recognized, but because I apparently had the power to get this man out of his seat.

"Hi, guys," I said to them. They smiled uncertainly until the man reappeared. In his hand he had three scraps of paper. He handed me the one with the phone number along with a grubby pen. The two other scraps he handed to the kids.

"Get this here guy's autograph," he told them. "He's a football player."

I knocked out two autographs for the kids on the side of the post that supported the porch's sagging roof. The kids quietly thanked me. Armed with this goodwill, I pumped the man for information on any neighbors that might have been living there twenty-five years before.

"The only one been around here that long," he told me, "would be old Mrs. Evanston in that house over there. She's old enough. . . . "

I thanked the man and he returned to his nest on the porch, watching me curiously as I crossed the street to the only well-kept house on the block. The jet-black driveway had been paved within the past year, and a fresh coat of brown paint clashed incongruously with the electric blue shutters adorning the simple-looking ranch. There was a large picture window beside the front door. Through a translucent drape I could see the ghost of Mrs. Evanston. After I rang, she slowly got up off the couch and shuffled toward the door. The hardware rattled for a full minute before a wedge of her face appeared in the crack of the door underneath the safety chain. Her dark eyes were owlish, enlarged by a thick, round pair of glasses. Her face was pale and mottled with liver spots. Skin hung from her chin like leftover cookie dough.

"What do you want?" she said through the glass storm door with a malevolent glare.

"Mrs. Evanston? I'm Tim Green," I told her, shamelessly rattling off a thumbnail sketch of my football career in hopes of getting past the chain, if not the storm door.

She considered me a moment, and then her face softened a bit. "I've heard of you," she said, closing the door momentarily before opening it wider, this time without the chain.

Then, not unkindly, she asked, "What do you want?"

With a blatant play on her likely sympathies, I told her that I was looking for my mother from whom I was separated at birth. I recounted what I knew of Joanne's history and asked her if she recalled such a woman about twenty-five years ago.

"I know it was a long time," I told her, "but I just thought that by chance you might remember something."

"I think I might remember," she told me after a moment.

My heart quickened.

"Seems to me she was a nice enough young girl, and a nice enough young man, too," she said. "But I can't remember all that much about them, just that they were there. . . . "

"Nothing at all?" I prompted.

She thought for a few more minutes, working her brow up and down and murmuring to herself as she concentrated on the floor.

"No," she rattled, looking up. "Nothing."

"Is there anyone else around who might have remembered them, Mrs. Evanston?"

"No, there's no one else." Then she added defiantly, "This neighborhood didn't used to be like this."

"I appreciate your time, Mrs. Evanston," I told her. "If you happen to remember anything in the next couple of days, or even weeks from now, I'd really appreciate it if you'd call me."

I took a scrap of paper from inside my jacket and wrote down my name and number.

"You're really the football player, aren't you?" she said, retrieving the scrap of yellow paper through the small crack she'd opened between the glass storm door and its aluminum frame.

"Yes ma'am," I said to her, displaying better manners than I really had. "Thank you."

I crossed the street and got into the truck beside Illyssa, reporting to her my findings.

"Look at this street," I said to her as I backed out of the driveway waving to the man on the porch, "it's a dump."

"Maybe it wasn't always like this," she said hopefully.

"That's what the lady said."

"What are you going to do now?" Illyssa asked.

"Keep going," I told her. "It's like football. You run play after play after play, and then all of a sudden maybe you break loose and score. It's like I can feel it now, knowing she was here. . . . "

She nodded.

"I'm going to do what Al Miller said. I'll go to the library and look in the community directories. Maybe Ed Burgen will be in there. It might list his occupation or even his company. Then I could track him down through his work. Or there might be other people who lived in this neighborhood who might have known them."

"And the landlord," she reminded me. "Who knows? The person who rented it back then might be the same person who rents it now. They might have records. . . . "

There was a lot I could do, and it felt good to be on the trail. The hardest part had been getting myself to start.

"There was a doctor's name on that medical report, too," I told her. "I'm going to find him and ask him. Maybe he has his own records on my mother."

"Would he give them to you?"

I shrugged. "It depends on how big of a football fan he is."

Twenty-eight

For the next three months, I searched. I spent almost as many hours in the city's public library as I did in the law library at the university. I continued to train my body for football and write. Our wedding was approaching fast, and it appeared that it would take place without my mother being there to see it. I wanted her to see it. It signified not only the high degree of happiness that I had been able to attain, but the social distance I had traveled from 116 Putman Street.

Illyssa's father paid for the entire affair. There were three hundred people invited, and it was held at the East River Yacht Club in New York on a pier that jutted into the river. The breathtaking Manhattan skyline unfolded behind towering arrangements of flowers. People arrived driving Rolls-Royces and Mercedes and long black limousines that they actually owned. Women were laden with diamonds and jewels. The food was sublime. (I ate five entrees.) Every table was a unique invention in floral design. It was a scene I had only previously experienced in books like *The Great Gatsby;* it was nothing I had ever seen in all my past experiences.

Kyle showed up with his girlfriend from Atlanta. He looked like a movie star in his rented tuxedo with his long hair pulled back and the buxom blond Southern belle on his arm. Illyssa's girlfriends from school marveled at his physical beauty. I marveled that he'd somehow scraped together enough money to get there and also manage to rent a tuxedo. I was glad to see Kyle, though, and proud of how far he'd come.

The day after we were married we left for our honeymoon in Europe. From Venice, we went to the Amalfi Coast, then to Rome, and finally Paris. It was magic, and during those sixteen days I forgot, maybe for the first time, about all the aspirations that had previously driven me through life. I relaxed completely and enjoyed the first two and a half weeks with my new wife as if they were the beginning of life itself. I took special pleasure in referring to Illyssa as "my wife," whether we were selecting a Venetian vase for our dining room or choosing a bottle of wine for dinner. I doted and talked so endlessly about "my wife" that I'm sure the Italians thought I was touched. I suppose I was, and for that matter, I still am—at least when it comes to my wife.

When we returned home, we were soon confronted with the fact that Illyssa was not pregnant. I know it's ludicrous now, but it sent me into a state of complete panic then. We had decided that we would begin having children right away. My plan was that she would get pregnant on our honeymoon. The fact that she didn't prompted me to irrationally suppose that I wouldn't be able to have kids. I implored Illyssa to make an immediate appointment with her doctor so that we could proceed with the proper tests and medical treatments to alleviate the problem if it was at all humanly possible.

Within a week, we found ourselves sitting face-to-face with Illyssa's doctor. Her office was spacious but austere. It was a place filled with books and papers, a place for work. She was a pleasant woman from India with Western features and long thick hair that was darker than a crow's wing but without its iridescence. She was completely mystified over the whole thing.

"We want to have children," I explained. "I think I need to be tested to see if that's possible. Do you think I could do that right away?"

"Mr. Green," she explained patiently in her thick accent, "it takes most normal couples between six months to a year to conceive a child. You have only been trying for a few weeks. I think you should continue to have normal relations and let nature take its course. There is no need to be tested at this point in time. . . . "

She looked sympathetically at Illyssa and then back to me. It was quite evident to her that the problem lay somewhere in my mind.

"You don't understand," I told them both. The words escaped from my throat like the groans of a tortured man. "I don't know where I came from . . . I don't know if I'll leave anything behind. I'm like a spark from a campfire, flying up into the black night. . . . If I can't have kids then there's nothing after me. I'm like the spark, coming from nothing, leaving nothing, a meaningless flicker with nothing before it and nothing after. . . . "

I looked hard to see if they understood this. The doctor was obviously disconcerted. Illyssa, I could tell, felt bad for me. She knew what was burning deep down inside me. She knew that my feelings of disconnection sprung from my adoption and that I was distracted by the notion of being nothing more than a single point rather than part of some continuing line. For the same reason, to outlive one's own children is a universally age-old curse. No one wants to feel as if they've left nothing behind. Illyssa reached across the space between our two hands and squeezed mine.

"It will be all right," she said. "She knows. Listen to her. Let's give it time."

I defiantly wiped the corners of my eyes. I wasn't embarrassed for feeling the way I did. If I couldn't find where I'd come from, it was obviously imperative to leave some genetic imprint of myself behind. If I couldn't be the continuum of a traceable bloodline, then I was desperate to be the beginning of my own.

I have driven my wife crazy about many things since the first day we met, but probably no topic could match the frequency with which I harped on that one. Thankfully for her—I had become intolerable—it became apparent during the next month that she was indeed pregnant. I was ecstatic.

Before we knew it, the summer had escaped and we were packing our things once again to move back to Atlanta for the football season. I was no closer to finding my mother, but I carried with me a certainty now that it would somehow happen. The key was in the hands of Al Miller.

At the beginning of every NFL season during August training

camp, when the teams are sequestered to endure five weeks of brutal practices, there is a mandated meeting between the FBI and NFL security with every NFL team. The main purpose of this meeting is to warn players away from the vices of drugs and gambling, as well as to inform them of the latest and greatest confidence schemes being used to blackmail players or otherwise steal their money.

The Falcons organization holds its team meetings during training camp in a series of interconnected wooden bungalows immediately adjacent to the Falcon Inn, where we lived during camp. It was ten minutes before our annual meeting with the FBI and NFL security when Al Miller found me hobbling slowly toward the meeting room. I had a bruise on my kneecap and was dragging my leg along behind me like a post. I would have preferred to be back in my room with my knee packed in ice and my leg elevated by way of a dresser drawer I'd stuck underneath the mattress at the end of my bed. I was already familiar with the FBI's stories about gambling, bookies, drugs, and mobsters, since they varied little from year to year.

The most infamous malefactor on the FBI's list was Dr. Buedrow. Every year Buedrow seemed to lure one athlete or another into his snares and then attempt to extort money from him. Buedrow would show up at a hotel bar with a beautiful woman he claimed to be his daughter. The daughter would then seduce the athlete and Buedrow would escort them to a suite in the hotel. There, Buedrow would slip something into the unsuspecting player's drink. The player would inevitably wake up groggy and find himself in a compromising position, not with Buedrow's alleged daughter, but with another man. There were always photos. Blackmail ensued.

Besides an update on Buedrow's latest tricks, I couldn't have been less interested in what the FBI had to say. But in football, you go where you're told when you're told. It doesn't always have to make sense.

"Hi, Al. Did they catch him yet?" I said, pulling up alongside Al Miller, who was leaning against the wall outside the meeting room with his hands stuffed in his pockets.

"Hello, Tim," he returned, smiling in his ever-cheerful manner. "Who?"

"Buedrow, the doctor. Have they nailed him yet?"

Al's face grew long and serious as he shook his head, obviously disappointed with his former team.

"They haven't seemed to," he said.

"Well," I said with a shrug, "it gives everybody something to think about."

He nodded at that, happy to see that I wasn't condemning anyone. "Tim," he said under his breath, taking my arm and pulling me close, "you know Bernard Lincoln, don't you?"

I had no idea.

"He's the director of NFL security," Al told me patiently. "He's my boss. He came for tonight's meeting. I was thinking that maybe you could say something to him, tell him what you're trying to do. . . . If he gives me his approval, I could use some of our other people around the NFL to help us. I told him a little about what you're trying to do, but if you would just say something to him, it could really help us out. . . . "

I've never been above asking for favors, and I was grateful that Al was considering the situation from the perspective of "us." He led me straight to the man who was his boss. Bernard was a light-skinned African-American who seemed disinterested in my story. His face hung from the bones beneath his skin as if he were on the verge of sleep. When the outline of my story was finished, however, he told me he thought NFL security could be of help.

I thanked him just as the meeting was being called to order by the head coach. I sat down with the rest of the team to watch a slide show that included a series of coke mules whose caches had exploded in their intestines, leaving them twisted and tortured with foam erupting from their frozen mouths. I listened carefully to stories about kidnappings and cement shoes and wondered just what it was that Al Miller had in mind. It was obvious that he had some plan. Al may have looked like somebody's doting grandfather, but I knew for a fact that he'd survived a lot of the real-life crap being projected onto the big screen in the front of the darkened room.

■■■

Within a week, Al had more good news. With clearance from Bernard, he'd enlisted the help of Melvin Rowe, the New York Jets security man who'd run the DMV check on Joanne for us last spring. It seems Melvin, with the new directive from Bernard, was ready to tap some of his sources in Albany. Since we knew from my noniden-tifying information that my mother was married in the eighth month of her pregnancy, and since we knew that her last name was Burgen at the time of my birth and the name of my father listed on the med-ical record was Edward, we reasoned that Joanne had married Edward Burgen somewhere in the state of New York in November of 1963.

We needed a New York State marriage license. That would tell us not only Joanne's maiden name, but the birthplace of both Joanne and Ed Burgen. I had spent time that summer randomly calling the directory information of different area codes, then calling every list-ing of Edward Burgen, of which there were often more than one. The problem with directory information is that an increasing number of people have their numbers unlisted. It was certainly possible that I had already asked for the Ed Burgen who'd married my mother, but had been denied his number. The information on a marriage license would focus the scope of our search. The birthplaces of both Ed and Joanne would very likely still possess relatives with the same last names, if not Joanne and Ed themselves. Of course, marriage licenses are not readily available. But Melvin had been high enough up in the Albany DA's office that he still had some pull in the capital. It would take him a few months, but by January, without telling us how, he would deliver the essential document.

Twenty-nine

That winter, after another failing football season for the Falcons, Illyssa and I went to the New York City area instead of returning home to Liverpool. I was enrolled at the Cardozo Law School in Manhattan and Illyssa, six months pregnant, was gleeful at the prospect of living with her mother in the place she'd grown up and where she would deliver her own first child. To complete my unorthodox pursuit of a law degree, I needed to take some first-year classes that Syracuse University only offered in the fall, but which Cardozo conveniently offered in the spring semester.

Susan Wolkoff, Illyssa's mom, lived in Hewlett, one of the Five Towns on the south shore of Long Island, about forty-five minutes from Manhattan. I would ride the Long Island Railroad into Penn Station every day and then take a subway downtown to Cardozo. It was about an hour and fifteen minutes each way to get to and from my classes, but living out in Hewlett was worth the commute. There was a tranquillity in my mother-in-law's neighborhood that seemed unattainable on the island of Manhattan.

I was never free from my need to work out. Lifting weights and running were as constant in my life as eating and breathing. So I trained at a nearby gym where the manager, a Columbia Ph.D. student, let me in for free since I was an NFL player. To fulfill my two daily miles of roadwork, I would wend my way through the opulent winding streets of Hewlett Harbor where my mother-in-law's house rested among carefully manicured lawns, shrubs, and trees. Despite all the money I had made as an NFL player, these homes left me with much to aspire to.

We had barely settled in at my mother-in-law's when I got a call from my brother Kyle. He was ready for a career change, and he needed some money. His plan was to accompany his girlfriend back to her hometown in Brunswick, Georgia. Apparently they had both run out of luck in Atlanta and she assured him that better things waited for them in the southern part of the state. Kyle always had an affinity for the ocean, so he was more than glad to go along.

Besides that, he had lost the job I'd helped him get with the trucking company. Apparently he'd been delivering a load of paper to a warehouse in Los Angeles when things started to go wrong. Bad luck hit first when no one arrived at the appointed warehouse to unload the trailer. Kyle patiently explained to me how he called everyone he could think of, but got through to no one. He spoke like a man who'd spent countless years on the road about a situation that was obviously intolerable. Exasperated, because driving a big rig around the city streets of Los Angeles was so disconcerting, even to a veteran trucker, he finally left the trailer with its load of paper along a random side street somewhere within the Los Angeles city limits.

"If those stupid sons of bitches weren't going to tell me where I was supposed to go," he told me, "I wasn't going to keep driving around L.A. with a big trailer. Sooner or later I would have gotten a ticket and that's the last thing you want on your driving record. . . . "

I asked him if he didn't think a ticket on his record might look a little better than an abandoned load of paper products.

"See," he said, "there you go. You look at it the same damn way they do. . . . I can't talk to you about it. . . . "

He continued to talk, however. I think more than anything, he wanted to get the whole thing off his chest. He knew I'd listen, even if I couldn't help offering up my own distorted wisdom from time to time.

He drove around for a while after lightening his load, hoping he'd find the correct warehouse and stopping every so often to use a pay phone to call into his home base back in Georgia. When he finally got a hold of a dispatcher, things got nasty. The dispatcher, whose name was Kelvin, told him he'd broken every company rule by leaving his load at an undesignated location.

My brother was personally offended by Kelvin's words and hung up abruptly. He found his trailer again, hooked it up, and delivered it promptly to the warehouse he'd been at in the first place. This time the appropriate workers were there to meet him. Immediately after dropping off his load, he started his journey back across the width of the continent with the idea that he'd show Kelvin a thing or two when they were face-to-face. Kelvin, a forty-two-year-old alcoholic with a Louisiana accent and a broken front tooth, was a big, heavyset man, but Kyle was a street fighter, and he figured if he met up with the older dispatcher late enough into the day, he'd be drunk enough so that Kyle could kick his ass around the depot without getting much more than some scratches on his knuckles.

Unfortunately for Kyle, the big Kenworth tractor he was driving took ill over the Rockies and flat broke down not too far inside the Arizona border. He used his CB radio to arrange for a tow. At the nearest truck stop, a seventeen-year-old Indian kid with a greasy pompadour told him they needed $260 to replace his diesel manifold. This was about all the money my brother had to his name, so he called in to his company. Unfortunately, it was Kelvin who answered the call, and he continued to give Kyle a hard time. In a disdainful tone, he recited the company policy that required Kyle to use his own money for minor repairs. He would be reimbursed in his next paycheck.

At that point, Kyle figured that he had about enough to either fix the truck or buy a bus ticket home with enough change left over to eat steak and eggs all the way back to the East Coast. In his own mind, it was an easy decision to abandon both the broken tractor and his driving career at that roadside stop somewhere in the Arizona desert. The only things he regretted was the paycheck he'd earned but wasn't going to collect and the fact that Kelvin was going to get through the week without the good ass-kicking he deserved.

For all his toughness, though, Kyle would never return to the trucking company depot. It wasn't fear of a good fight that kept him away, either. Kyle was never one to shy away from a physical confrontation, and in that way I always admired him. Outside the football field I tended to shy away from those types of situations. But where my timidity lay in the physical realm, his lay in the psychological one. To face the outrage of the manager, who, by the way, was the man who'd given him the job in the first place, was as unthinkable to Kyle as walking into the depot and busting Kelvin was to me.

No, it was certainly much easier for Kyle to call me and get a temporary loan for enough lawn equipment to start up a company of his own once he hit Brunswick. Things this time, he assured me, were going to be much different. He would be working by himself, for himself. There would be no one else he would have to depend on to get things done the right way and no one around to screw him the way the trucking company so obviously had.

The day after I sent Kyle a check to begin his life anew in Brunswick, I got a call from Al Miller. His man had come through in a big way. Al read me the information on the marriage certificate the way a grade school kid might read off the marks from a perfect report card.

"It's all here," he said finally, "you'll be able to find her now. . . . "

"I should," I said, and then thanked him profusely.

My mother and her husband had both been born in Cleveland. The name of both Ed's and Joanne's parents were listed on the certificate. The maiden name of my mother's mother was Heathslide. That was unusual enough to make it relatively easy for someone who knew what they were doing to track down a relative of Joanne's if one of the Heathslide clan was still alive.

When I got the information from Al, I didn't act on it immediately. I knew I could find my mother now, and that gave me a certain sense of relief. The information I had was too powerful and too specific for me not to be able to track her down. Yet I hesitated. Suddenly I was unsure. With the prospect of finding her so close at hand, I was afraid. After all, she had never registered with the state of New York, so how serious could she have been about finding me? Also, my friend Stu's warnings rang in my mind. Maybe I should leave well enough alone. What if Joanne turned out to somehow be another Martha-type situation?

Not only could it be that she was disinterested, it was certainly possible that Joanne might be offended that I had tracked her down and found her after all these years. It was possible that she would slam the door in my face. The notion of having built myself up so carefully for twenty-six years only to remain unwanted and cast aside once again like a broken pot gave me much to consider. After my frantic search, I became suddenly judicious. I wanted to think about the situation a little before plunging headlong into what were unfathomable waters. I wanted to brace myself in the event that beneath the surface there was nothing more than jagged, unyielding rocks.

My brother-in-law's best friend's mom was a private detective. After the appropriate incubation period, where the certainty that my mother would love me outgrew any doubts I might have had, I asked her to shag down a Cleveland Heathslide or two and see if she couldn't come up with Joanne's whereabouts. The next evening, after returning home from my classes in the city, she called to give me Joanne's phone number in Philadelphia. A Heathslide aunt fell for the ruse of an old schoolmate looking for a girlfriend who had once been Joanne Sloan, but who married a man by the name of Ed Burgen immediately after graduation.

"She got it," I said, laying down the phone in a catatonic state.

"What are you going to do?" Illyssa asked me.

I stared blankly at her, but even before the words left my mouth, I was dialing the phone.

"I'm going to call her," I said.

Thirty

When I dialed the number, I got a taped message saying that it was no longer working in that area code. I tried it again.

"It doesn't work," I agonized, hearing the same message.

"Try again," said my wife.

I did. Same thing. Then I called information to find out what had happened to that number. The directory assistant told me that many of the area codes in the Philadelphia area had been changed. I should try 942 instead of 215.

My fingers trembled, and I felt that out-of-body quality that I had only experienced before when wrestling free from the grip of a particularly violent blow to the head during a football game. It was the sensation of being a balloon, tethered to something solid but only by the thinnest line.

"Do you want me to go?" Illyssa asked.

We were in the den on the ground floor of the house. It was a cavernous room. Dark night flooded in through the windows, fought back by a single dim lamp next to the couch. I waved to her in the offhand way of a drunk who doesn't understand the question. I dialed the correct number, vaguely aware that Illyssa had left the room, not to abandon me, but to let me make the connection without distraction.

It rang three times before I heard the melodious voice of a woman who sounded much too young to be my mother.

"Hello?" she said, soft but clear and cheerful, like the distant sound of a rural church bell on a winter's night.

"Hello?" I said, choking out the second syllable.

"Hello?" she said, puzzled now.

"Is this Joanne?" I asked.

"Yes," she said in a whisper, as if she were hearing the voice of a ghost, although she had no idea that she really was.

I took a deep breath. My chest shuddered as it filled and emptied.

"Who is this?" she said finally, still quiet, still sweet.

"I'm your son," I told her. Every muscle in my body shook at that moment. I had no idea what it would be like to be there in that instant, talking to my mother for the first time in my life. I never knew for certain if it would ever even happen. But there I was, drifting helplessly amid a current too powerful to even comprehend.

She said nothing then, and there was silence for a long time.

"Are you there?" I said, but she had gone. No one answered.

"Are you there?" I tried again, desperate for her to have not cut the line, an act that would undoubtedly extinguish a vital part of my soul. But still there was nothing.

"If you're there," I said, "please just say something, anything . . . if you're still there. I need to know if you're there."

"I'm here," she said, so faintly that I wondered if it had only been my imagination.

"Do you want me to tell you who I am?" I said, grabbing a handful of hair on my forehead.

"Yes," she whispered.

Then I told her. I told her who I was and what I was. I listed everything I'd done to that date, rolling accomplishments off the end of my tongue like a salesman selling the fastest-moving model on the lot. My pitch was practiced and concise, not that I'd ever said those words before, but I'd thought them. I realize now that I had been stockpiling my ceaseless list of achievements for that exact moment.

From the time I could first think, I began preparing myself. I would be so impressive, so irresistible, that there was no way my mother could do anything but listen in amazement, wonder, and admiration.

Then, finally, she would adore me. She would want to know more about who I was and how I had come to be so outstanding. She would want to stake a claim on me, to call part of me her own. She would want to take some credit, even if secretly, for who and what I was.

That was what I wanted, and as I heard myself spew forth all the things I was, all the things I had done, I believed that I would be impossible for her to resist. In truth, the only thing that gave me any anxiety whatsoever was the fact that I had not yet published a novel. Everything else, it seemed to me, I had: academic excellence, athletic prowess, wealth, a measure of fame that was likely to grow, health, happiness, a wife I loved, a child on the way, friends I adored, experience, manners, potential . . . only the title of author remained uncertain. Lawyer was sure to come. That was nothing more than a merit badge in the making.

"I'm writing a book, too," I said hesitantly. "It's not finished, but it will be soon. I want to be a writer. It's something I can do the rest of my life, when football is over."

"Your . . . parents must be very proud of you," Joanne said after I finally stopped.

"Yes," I said, "they are . . . very."

Then, without hesitation, as if it was the next most logical and natural question (and maybe it was) I said, "Who is my father?"

My mother responded in kind, as if I'd asked nothing more than what the weather was supposed to be the next morning.

"You're father's name is Don Reinwulf," she told me. "I met him in college, but I haven't seen or heard from him since I was in school."

"What school?" I said. I had no idea if at the end of our conversation Joanne was going to pull up stakes and move to Pago Pago without a trace. I didn't think so, but I just didn't know, so I wanted to get as much information as I could. It was certainly conceivable that I might never speak to her again. I had caught her off guard, and like a prudent general, I knew I should advance as far as possible before there was an opportunity to mount a resistance.

Joanne told me where both she and my father had gone to school. She told me the circumstances under which they'd met and how they'd parted with my father's disdainful refusal to accept the fact that she was pregnant.

"I had nowhere to go," she explained in a voice that still sounded to me like that of a much younger woman. "I had no money. My mother had no money. My father didn't live with us, and he didn't have much to do with me. The only person I could turn to was Ed. He and I were best friends in high school. He was working as an electrical engineer in Syracuse. He told me to go there and that he'd take care of me. . . . I was a teacher, but in my situation, there was no way I would have even been able to get a job. It was different then."

She told me about Ed and about the two children they had several years after I was born, a girl and a boy, my half sister and half brother, Mary and Kenny. Suddenly, there was more than one person to whom I was genetically attached. She told me that she worked as the director of education in a children's hospital in Philadelphia.

I told her about my parents, how they'd raised me, the values they'd instilled in me, about how I wasn't afraid to work hard to get things, that they'd taught me that. I told her about my brother Kyle and my sister. I told her all about Illyssa, how we'd met, and the names we'd picked out for our baby if it was a boy or a girl.

We talked for almost two hours before she finally said she had to go. She left for her office every morning at five. I would have talked for two weeks if I could have. It was an incredibly pleasurable experience for me to recount for her every last detail of my life. The only way Joanne could get me off the line was to promise she'd call me the next day. We said goodnight, and I hung the phone up slowly and thoughtfully.

Illyssa and her mother were in the kitchen, waiting for me. I told them everything and worried out loud about whether or not Joanne would really call me back.

"Of course she will," they both said, but it certainly seemed to me then that it was possible she might not. As sweet as her voice had sounded, it seemed to me that she might very well decide that, since we had both done well going our separate ways, it would also be the best course for our futures. I knew now who my mother was, but it was like many other things in my life: Once I had a hold of what I'd set out for, I found I wanted more. Now I wanted to know not just who she was, but to know her like a son. I wanted her to feel the same way about me as she so obviously did about my brother Kenny and my sister Mary. I could no more help myself from wanting that than I could any of the things I had wanted in life. It came from within and it consumed me.

Thirty-one

During our two-hour conversation, I didn't do all the talking. Joanne told me about her life as well. She was born in 1940. Her father, James Sloan, a surly Irishman, had been at times a minor league baseball player as well as a policeman. But Joanne never had much of a chance to call him her own. He was married to another woman even before my mother was born. My grandmother, it seemed, was a loving but unconventional sort of woman who took my grandfather's shortcomings in stride. In fact, she felt sorry for him.

The reality of the situation was that my grandfather's legal wife had been institutionalized. Being a devout Catholic, he was averse to divorcing his stricken wife. He was not, however, devout enough to keep himself from falling in love with, and into the bed of, another woman, namely my grandmother. Against the wishes of her own mother and anyone who had her ear, my grandmother took up with James Sloan and soon the two of them were living together.

Unfortunately, when my mother was four years old, her father's legal wife recovered from her illness and was released from the institution where everyone had erroneously presumed she would spend the rest of her life. James, my grandfather, was seized by a sudden sense of duty, and, I presume, he had begun to feel burdened by the woman and the child they had conceived out of wedlock. So like men throughout history, he returned home, the repentant husband, leaving a wake of destruction in his path that he felt little need of attending to after his redemption. He hadn't really died in an auto-mobile accident, but he was as good as dead to Joanne.

It was, in fact, my grandfather's legal wife who showed as much concern for my mother as anyone during her childhood. My grand-mother was not one for living alone, and by the time my mother was eleven, she found herself another man, this time an unmarried one, who she staked a legal claim to. My mother's stepfather was cruel and uncaring in ways reminiscent of children's fairy tales. He belit-tled her at every opportunity. In his eyes, she could do nothing right. She was born of sin and there she would remain. Only my mother's unwavering optimism and internal fortitude carried her through.

Like many women in that situation, my grandmother split her affections between the two of them, carefully preserving the appear-ance to her husband that he wasn't being neglected because of some-one else's illegitimate child while loving my mother on the side. My mother's own grandmother lived nearby, but she was of no comfort at all. She was a strict Victorian woman who never sought to soften the fact that Joanne was an illegitimate child in a time when children were held accountable for their parents' transgressions.

Luckily, my mother was a pretty girl. She had that, as well as being smart, to help her along. Also, she had the knack, which I know I inherited from her directly, of pleasing all but the most incorrigible people who fell into her life's path. The only one she never seemed able to please was her stepfather. Only I know, since I think much the same way she does, how hard Joanne must have tried. She grew up much the same as I had, constantly trying to secure the love and admiration of not just her family but of even the strangers sitting next to her on the bus. And like me, she lived with the constant awareness that somehow her existence was the result of a mistake.

Unlike me, Joanne didn't have a solid family structure with a clear-cut mother and father who would allow her to assail the world and be judged solely on her merits. Joanne was a marked child, and I think it was something that was burned so deeply into her conscious-ness that it affects her even today. She told me that every Sunday when she walked into the church, she was acutely aware of the stares and whispers in her wake.

Still, she managed. She did well in school and became a member of the band. During high school, she began dating Edward, whose father owned the local pharmacy. They would go their separate ways when it came time to go to college. He went to a university in Philadelphia and my mother had to go to the only place that would provide her with a loan for tuition, the University of Akron. In fact, when she left for school the summer after she turned nineteen, Joanne had only enough money for a one-way ticket to Akron and a few meals once she arrived, nothing more.

Still, she felt liberated. My mother loved books and learning and, just as important, she realized that an education would empower her like nothing else in her life ever had before. She knew that with a college degree she could separate herself from the inauspicious beginnings that were no fault of her own. She set out to get a degree in education, intent on becoming a teacher herself. To pay for school, she worked as a nanny for a family that lived in a suburb of Akron. It was her job to help cook and clean and care for three children at the same time she was attending classes.

Working her way through college this way afforded Joanne little time for socializing. She didn't drink. She didn't smoke. She rarely had time to go out on dates. Most of the adventure and romance my mother experienced was through the books she never stopped reading.

And so it was that my mother observed my father at the university for a long time before she ever said a single word to him. He was tall and handsome and viciously independent. Besides being a basketball player and mathematics major, he was also in the ROTC, so when he graduated, he would become an officer in the army. From the stories she'd read, my mother knew that some men, no matter how apparently incorrigible, were only a good woman away from respectability and happiness. Although my father was a carousing drinker and womanizer, my mother suspected that if he ever knew her, really knew her, she could change his ways. It wasn't hard for her to envision the two of them living out some splendid romance worthy of her finest novels.

These, however, were sentiments of which my father was completely unaware. Because of some of my own self-indulgent behavior during college, I can easily understand how my father's thought process went. Here was a girl who was attractive and naive, too quiet to be alluring, but, if thrown into his path at the right moment, was the perfect tonic for a night on the town.

My father was a year older than my mother and had actually graduated from the university when they first encountered one another face-to-face. He was visiting some friends for a last time before being shipped to Germany on assignment. My mother hadn't seen him in quite some time. She'd all but forgotten her wistful fantasies. She was in her final year of school, with thoughts of soon becoming a teacher. It would be the first time in her life she would be free from need.

She fell into his path in a moment of weakness. School had been particularly difficult. Her work as a housekeeper and nanny had grown extremely tiresome. Uncertainties about the future loomed. It was rare for my mother to be out at night in a bar, but when some classmates pressed her to join them on that particular night, she acquiesced. She had a drink, which she was completely unused to doing. She had another. It was too much. My father was out that same night at the same place. He was drunk, a condition quite familiar to him at the time.

For Joanne, the people and the noise and smoke all ran together, as if she were looking up at everything from the bottom of a swimming pool. There was a quiet peacefulness in that din and she gave herself up to it. Then he was there, in front of her, smiling in his rakish, practiced way. To her, it appeared that he was simply a part of some romantic dream, one that was destined to play itself out since the beginning of time.

I believed her the first time she told me that she didn't remember the rest, and I believe her now. I don't know if her amnesia was induced by alcohol or her own powerful ability to suppress unwanted memories, but all the same, I'm sure it's true. She only knew later that she had been compromised, and she remembered my father.

Nothing like that had happened to my mother before, so when she learned that she was pregnant, she also knew by whom. She confronted my father in a sober moment, only days before he was to leave the country. He scoffed at her, suggesting that if in fact she was pregnant, it certainly must have been at the hands of some other man. Humiliated and helpless, but too proud to attach herself to him, my mother never spoke another word. She pressed her lips together and, instead of crying, devised a plan.

Thirty-two

My mother did call me the next day. What I felt was too deeply rooted inside me to describe with words—or to fully understand, for that matter. Suffice it to say that the thrill of finding her was small by comparison to the knowledge that I would not lose her again. That knowledge came with her call.

I had spent the day in Manhattan sitting through classes on contracts, torts, and constitutional law without hearing a word. The train ride back out to Long Island seemed to take forever, and by the time I finally got to the Hewlett station, the dark skies had begun to spill heavy drops of rain. I slogged four blocks to Susan's house without feeling a thing. Illyssa greeted me expectantly at the door.

"She called," Illyssa said breathlessly, and my heart leapt. Illyssa took my jacket from me as I kicked off my wet sneakers and made my way downstairs to the abandoned den without bothering to put on the lights.

I called Joanne at home and spoke to her for over an hour. I surprised myself with the torrent of details I had yet to tell her about my life. Things I hadn't remembered the day before were suddenly there, flowing forth with the more memorable parts of my history. My entire life was replayed in my mind in fast sequence. Joanne listened patiently and with understanding, knowing instinctively how important it was to me that she knew everything that had happened. After some time, my jaw actually grew weary and the flow of my words slowed to a stop. I was alone in my mother-in-law's den sitting sprawled out on the couch in the quiet darkness of that big empty room. Joanne cleared her throat quietly, then wondered aloud how it was that I was not overwrought with anger and resentment.

I laughed flippantly, as if the sound of my laugh alone was explanation enough. Still she waited.

"Don't you understand?" I said passionately. "Everything worked out just the way it should have. I couldn't be happier! I've had a great life. Look where I am. Look at the things I've been able to do. Look at the things I can still do. Everything was possible, only because of the decision that you made. . . . "

"I didn't want you to grow up the way I did," she whispered. "I didn't want that for you. . . . "

"I know that," I told her eagerly. I didn't want her to feel guilt. I didn't want to repel her in any way.

"I'm glad you did what you did," I told her. "Don't you see?"

I'm certain that my words didn't completely dissuade Joanne from suspecting that I harbored at least some subconscious resentment. I think that by now, more than seven years later, her concerns have been allayed, but it took all that time. In her own mind, she couldn't imagine my not taking her to task for leaving me in the hands of someone else, no matter how capable those hands were. Because of the way my own parents had raised me—to examine every situation in its brightest light—it never occurred to me to think of Joanne as anything but wise for placing me with a family where I would not only be wanted and loved, but where I would not have to wear the emblem of illegitimacy around my neck the way that she had.

For the time being, we let that subject rest. Then I asked Joanne a question to which I thought I already knew the answer.

"Did you think about me?" I said, expecting a flood of emotion from my mother about sleepless nights and restless silent moments throughout the last twenty-six years during which she thought of nothing but me, where I was, how I was, who I was.

"No, I didn't think about you. After I knew you were in a good home, I didn't think about you at all," she told me, and it pierced my heart. The thing that had set my quest in motion from the start had been the torment that Audry, my old girlfriend's mother, felt at the inability to find her son. For six years, I had envisioned my own mother's torment at not knowing what had become of me. Now, to hear her say that she didn't think of me at all was shocking.

"Not at all?" I said in disbelief.

"You have to understand," she said softly. "After I did what I did, I had to block it from my mind. I did what I thought was best for you. Then I had to stop thinking about you. If I didn't, I wouldn't have been able to live with it. . . . "

This was something I needed to digest. Our conversation was hopelessly snagged, and Joanne had to make dinner for her family, half of whom had no idea yet that I even existed.

Joanne and Ed Burgen had not only stayed married for the past twenty-six years, they had raised my sister and brother with wonderful success. After the incident with me, my mother and her husband had gone on to live an enviable middle-class American life.

After working in the field of electrical engineering for different companies over the years, Ed opened his own business, which he still operates. Joanne wouldn't go to work at the children's hospital until after Kenny and Mary were in school. Both my brother and sister would go on to college and earn degrees in engineering. My brother would join a fraternity and play football. My sister would graduate with honors and then go on to get a master's degree in occupational therapy. My mother and her husband were understandably proud of not only their children, but the fact that they had somehow sculpted a blue-ribbon family from the ashes of a tragedy.

The fact that I now threatened the equilibrium of my mother's carefully constructed life was obvious. I suspected, however, that the accomplishments I had attained would soften the impact of my sudden appearance. It wasn't as if I were a shameful black sheep, coming back from the past to haunt my mother's existence with soiled hands. I wasn't a drug addict or a criminal. I wasn't even a malcontent. But still, for my mother, I was a hammer poised to shatter her carefully constructed life of middle-class respectability. She was afraid of how her children would react to my existence and the fact that she had hidden it from them. And I'm sure she was afraid of how I might react to them.

"I'm going to send you some pictures," Joanne said before she hung up. "I want you to see everyone."

I promised to do the same, and we agreed to talk the next day at the same time. I was happy that she was sending pictures, and glad to do the same in return. Still, the thing I wanted most was a subject that I had yet to broach with her. More than anything, I wanted to see her in person. I knew already from two telephone conversations that there were remarkable similarities in the way we thought and reacted to the world around us. But I needed to see her in person, to look into her eyes, face-to-face, and see what I could of myself.

Thirty-three

During the next few days, I spoke to Joanne as frequently as her schedule would allow. If she had fifteen minutes during the day, I would duck out of one of my law classes and call her on a pay phone. During those first few weeks, when I wasn't talking to Joanne, I was thinking about her. The only way I could sleep at night was to lose myself in the writing of my novel. In it, I had created a world full of characters with problems that were equally poignant, but far enough afield from my own so that sleep could overtake me in the early morning hours. I often fell asleep sitting at the desk in the empty bedroom of Illyssa's younger brother. Looking back, I think it's remarkable that Illyssa, who was seven months pregnant, never protested in the least. She never demanded or even asked for more attention. She simply stepped back and let the drama run its course.

When the photos of my mother and her family arrived, Illyssa scrutinized them with me, over and over, without any comment that wasn't positive and encouraging. It was a week after that before Joanne agreed to meet me in person. I think she wanted the pictures and the reality of everyone who was involved to sink in. It wasn't just her, she would tell me over and over again, she had a family that I would have to deal with as well. She was inseparable from her husband and children. If I wanted to have a relationship with her, that meant having one with them. She wanted me to fully digest that idea before charging ahead.

For several days after receiving the photos, I assured Joanne that her family would be a welcome part of my own. Again, it was my own parents' philosophy that love is anything but finite that enabled me to say that without hesitation. And so, Joanne agreed to meet me for lunch in Philadelphia fourteen days after I had first contacted her.

That morning, I put on a new sweater and some wool slacks and took my long, black leather trench coat from the closet. I wanted to look good without being formal. I wanted my mother to see me for the first time and realize that while my beginnings may have been ignoble, the end result was a paradigm of success and respectability unspoiled by haughtiness. Illyssa drove me to the airport and hugged me good-bye. She was more nervous for me than I was for myself. The shuttle to Philadelphia took only forty minutes, but I brought my laptop computer along with me anyway. As it is to this day, the ability to submerge my thoughts in writing acted like an opiate, obliterating the traumatic anxiety I would otherwise have felt. I think that to write well—or to read well for that matter—you must transport yourself into another time and place. Therein lies the opiate.

Of course, when we began our descent into Philadelphia, I had to turn the computer off. But by the time I completely returned from the lives of my characters, the wheels of the jet were slamming down onto the tarmac of Philadelphia International. When I got off the plane, my mother wasn't there. I choked down the bile of panic and proceeded toward the security checkpoint, reasoning to myself that some airports only let passengers proceed to the gates. The fact that other people were being greeted the moment they got off the plane made this charade difficult to carry out, but I have a good imagination, so I considered the possibilities.

Like many airports, the gates are separated from the main terminal by long, well-lit hallways. At the end of my hallway, a woman was coming toward me in a coat that was exactly the same as my own. As she came closer, I fought back the tears clouding my eyes. The person I was looking at was the mirror image of myself, in the form of a forty-nine-year-old woman. Even now, I can see her face as I first saw it. I could never forget it. Nor could I forget, or fully describe, the feeling when I first looked into the eyes of the woman from whom I was born.

To see oneself incarnate after searching for so long . . . to touch the hair that before was only your own . . . to feel the texture of the skin that no one else in your life had ever before possessed . . . to see the same nervous twitch in the corner of your eye . . . to sense the staccato inhalation of breath before speaking words full of emotion . . . to grasp hands that were shaped in the way of your own, just as strong, just as caring . . . are things that most people can never know.

Most people aren't adopted. For most people, the physical and psychological characteristics they share with their parents are indigenous. And for those who are adopted, most probably never find their biological mothers. For those who do, few, I doubt, will replicate them genetically the way I do my own mother. So for me, it was as if I had lived my life in darkness and could suddenly see.

I held my mother in that airport hallway for a long time and I cried with her for just as long. We cried for each other. We cried for ourselves. We cried for my parents. We cried for her family. And we cried for all the other adopted children out there, separated from something primal and something essential, who we knew would never feel what we were feeling at that moment.

I will never forget the first day I met Joanne. How could I? I'll never forget Anthony's on Liberty Avenue, where we ate lunch. I'll never forget the cold, gritty dirt of the streets and the screeching squeal of the trolley as we hustled from our parking space inside to the warm delicious smell of pizza and beer. I'll never forget the bright sunlight that spilled in through the slatted blinds as I wolfed down a hot roast beef sub with everything on it. Most of all, I'll never forget the fascination in seeing other people make the immediate connection between me and Joanne based solely on our appearances.

It was instant, and it was obvious. In fact, I can still see the olive-skinned man behind the counter at Anthony's wearing a white apron with the restaurant's name embroidered in bright red above his breast. I can see his five o'clock shadow and the flash of recognition in his nut-brown eyes that said, "Here is a man and his mother."

In fairness to Joanne, we weren't always suspected of being mother and son. Several months later, on one of her first visits to Syracuse, an acquaintance of mine who saw us at a restaurant, but knew nothing of my adoption, surreptitiously asked Illyssa if Joanne wasn't my older sister.

If life wasn't good enough then, it would only be a matter of weeks before Illyssa would go into labor with our first child, our son Cody. His middle name would be Raymond, after my mother Judy's father. Raymond Edinger, the proprietor of a country store in upstate New York, was the grandfather who taught me to drive a car and hunt and fish, a man adored not only by me but by everyone who ever knew him. As much as my reunion with Joanne meant to me, and as much of the mettle I was made of was directly attributable to her, I was determined to pay homage to the childhood that had forged me.

My son was a delight, and as with all my children, I took special pleasure in holding him close to me even before he was old enough to know the sound of my voice. Like all parents, I wanted to give Cody and the rest everything I never had. It wasn't material things I was concerned with, it was emotional. I seem to know with Cody how he feels. When he's afraid of the dark, I tell him it's all right, I was for most of my life. When he's embarrassed about his handwriting, I tell him he doesn't have to be, I had the same problem. I say these things without any disparagement toward my parents who raised me. There was no way they could fully understand my emotions the way I can understand my own children's. (Also, in no way do I mean to suggest that I'll know everything my children are ever thinking, just that there is a connection there that I never had.)

It was an incredible time for me. Within the period of eight weeks, for the first time in my life, I was able to lay my hands on the physical and spiritual essence of my future as well as my past. For some this might seem mundane, but for me, after having spent most of my life believing that I might never touch either one, it was a blessing that has been matched only by the day I was taken into the home of my parents and the day I met my wife, Illyssa.

Thirty-four

There were times during the next several months, as there were during the ensuing years, when everything didn't go quite as smoothly as one would have hoped or planned. But in all, the grafting of me and my life onto Joanne and her family's was a successful one.

We all met for the first time shortly after Cody was born. Mary, Kenny, and Ed welcomed the three of us openly. Kenny, himself a football player who was about to graduate from high school, was thrilled to learn that he had a brother who actually played in the NFL. Even at eighteen, he was kind enough and sensitive enough to our mother's apprehension to announce to everyone that he had always wanted an older brother. Years later, I would be proud to be the best man at his wedding. Mary fussed over the baby like a natural-born aunt. And Ed sat back, as he does to this day, observing, contemplating, and adding wisdom only after being consulted, but all the while generating a cheerful mood with his pleasant smile.

Of course, I still had my own family. I had no intention of altering the foundation that my world had been built upon. But because of the mutual aversion my brother Kyle and my parents shared for each other, I was already well versed at the social segregation of different units in the same family. My intent was to carry on with my parents as normal, allow my relationship with Joanne and her family to grow, and all the while keep the bulk of my energy and time focused on my wife and the tiny family we had just begun. Unfortunately, I wasn't successful on every count.

I suspect the rift that widened between me and my parents at that time was the result of two things. First, like anyone who feels guilt for having done something selfish that hurts someone else, I partially blamed my victims, who were my parents, for that guilt. Second, I think the hurt I caused my parents caused them to retract, probably in anticipation of future harm. Their retraction I took for repulsion. My blame they took for condemnation. Our estrangement escalated.

I never really told my parents that I had found Joanne, but I knew that they knew. What evolved was a perfunctory set of dinners accentuated by painfully tense holiday gatherings.

During these gatherings, my mother remained stiff, as if having been freshly offended by some rude remark. My father, who normally wore a complacent smile, was tight-lipped and tense. For my part, I would use the first possible excuse to depart. Illyssa was mystified. It wasn't that she hadn't experienced her share of turmoil growing up in a family split by divorce, it was that she'd never experienced such blatant repression on a firsthand basis.

My parents and I never spoke about what was wrong, but neither did we stop communicating. I remember the words of my tenth-grade history teacher. He told us that even a history of broken treaties were preferable to the alternative. He said that once two sides stopped talking, only war could follow. Tensions ran high between my parents and me, and there was no shortage of rattling sabers, but thankfully none of us declared war.

I finished the semester of law school in New York that spring, and we returned to Syracuse where I could pick up the intensity of my training for the upcoming football season.

One thing Joanne made me promise when she told me the story of my father was that if I ever did find him, I wouldn't ever talk about him to her or any of her family. I told her at the time that I had no immediate plans for that search, but over time that changed. Although the quest for my mother was certainly the thing that drove me through the events I have described in this story, the natural progression of my thoughts led inexorably to my father as well. Since I knew where both he and my mother had gone to school, and since I knew his name, it was a simple thing to call the alumni office at the school posing as a former graduate and ask for Don Reinwulf's current residence. He was listed at an address somewhere in the Seattle area.

Although I had his address that very summer, I didn't contact him. I was satisfied for the time being simply knowing where it was my father lived. Contacting him was something I could do at any time, and I would know when the time was right, I believed. Meanwhile, I focused on keeping my career as an NFL player afloat. During the off-season, the Falcons had fired the previous coaching staff and hired Jerry Glanville.

Glanville was the former head coach of the Houston Oilers, and although he led that team to four consecutive playoff appearances, he was known for leading a band of ruffians as well as wearing a black hat himself. Glanville is probably best known for leaving game tickets for Elvis at the will-call window of the Houston Astrodome. (By the way, Glanville and his bunch had renamed the Astrodome "The House of Pain.") In short, Jerry Glanville appeared to be the antithesis of everything I was accustomed to in the game of football.

When I learned Glanville was to be the head coach of my team, I remarked to Illyssa, "There's no way I'll ever fit in with a bunch of criminals."

"Who knows?" she told me. "Maybe Glanville and his guys aren't really criminals. And besides, maybe you'll win for a change."

She was right on both counts. Glanville, it turned out, was not only an excellent coach who led us to the playoffs in only his second year with the Falcons, he was a wonderful guy.

But during that summer I had no idea things would end up being as good as they did. That summer, I prepared for the worst. In a phone conversation from our home in Liverpool, I was told by Glanville that he was moving me back to the defensive line, the position I played in college. He said I would have to rely on quickness to survive, but if I could, he had just the position in his defense that I could not only play but thrive at. Only a guy who would leave tickets for Elvis would put a two-hundred-and-fifty-pound guy in the middle of an NFL defensive line.

I entered training camp that July in probably the best shape of my life. Glanville wanted me to be quick and able to run, and that's what I did. In fact, I ran so much during practice that my fellow defensive linemen became exasperated and asked me to slow down, since the coaches were starting to expect them to do the same. But I was intent on reforming my career, and if Glanville had asked me to dance in my jockstrap on the fifty-yard line, I probably would have.

By the end of August, I was showing promise as the smallest defensive lineman in the NFL, but the thing that really put me over the edge was a horribly bloody nose. We were in the middle of practice when an offensive lineman's finger got through the bars of my mask and halfway up my nose, tearing up my nasal cavity like metal cleats on wet grass. The blood roared from my nose, and I jogged to the sideline to get the trainers to stuff some cotton up there. In the midst of my medical attention, Glanville, who hadn't seen what happened, called for the next play to begin.

"Where the hell is ninety-nine?" he bellowed, calling me as he always did by number rather than name.

"He's getting fixed up by the trainers," one of the assistants said, pointing to the cluster of men surrounding me on the sideline.

"I guess she don't want to play that bad," Glanville said derisively, but before the words even left his mouth, I tore myself away from the trainers and was already halfway to the huddle.

"Don't you want to play, ninety-nine?" Glanville said in a high mocking voice.

"Yes," I said, taking my place in the middle of the huddle with my hands on my knees and looking straight ahead without a word about my nose.

Then Glanville leaned down and saw the blood. I was bleeding so profusely that the spaces between my teeth glimmered with crimson gore and each corner of my mouth as well as both nostrils bubbled merrily with fresh streams of blood.

"Hell, ninety-nine, you're bleeding like a stuck pig," Glanville said, serious now. "Go get that thing plugged."

"I'm fine," I told him, refusing to move. "I want to play."

A smile curled the corners of Glanville's lips ever so slightly and an elfin twinkle shone in his eyes.

"Ninety-nine!" he exclaimed, slapping me on the shoulder with great gusto. I think he would have preferred to see me disregard blood like that than gain four inches and fifty pounds.

That season, I would lead my team in quarterback sacks and have more tackles than any other lineman.

Just before camp broke, I saw Al Miller at our annual security meeting. I had called him during the spring to thank him for his help and let him know I'd found Joanne. He was thrilled when I spoke to him, but this was the first time I had seen him since last season. He greeted me with a broad smile and we shook hands warmly.

"How's everything with Joanne?" he asked right off.

"Great," I replied.

"And your parents?" he wanted to know.

"Good," I said cautiously, "but I've got a ways to go. I haven't really worked it out with them, you know?"

He frowned briefly, then said calmly, "They're the ones who raised you. Don't forget that."

Al had become like an uncle toward me during the past couple of years, so I wasn't offended by his gentle reminder.

I nodded. "I know. It will all work out."

"Good!" he said, as if the whole thing had been settled. "So, camp going well?"

"It's almost over," I said. "That's as good as it gets."

"But you're playing well," he said.

"It's going well. I seem to fit in with Jerry's defense."

"I'm glad for you," Al said.

"Al, I was wondering if you could do me another favor," I said. "God knows you've done enough, but I was wondering if you couldn't give me a hand with one more thing."

"Sure," he said. Al was the kind of guy who got excited when he could do something for you. Some people are happiest that way.

I told him that I had found where my father lived, but that I didn't know that much more about him. I explained the promise I'd made to my mother, and that I wanted to find out more about my father before I contacted him.

"I understand," he said, without my having to explain. "It's better that you find out some things about him before you just open yourself up, especially if you want to keep Joanne and her family separate. I'm sure he'll turn out to be a nice guy, but you just never know."

"So what do you think?" I said. "The guy with the Seahawks could help us, maybe?"

"That's exactly what I was thinking," Al told me with his knowing smile. "I'll have to check with Bernard Lincoln to get clearance, but I can't imagine he wouldn't say it was all right. I'll let you know."

Thirty-five

It was almost halfway through that football season before I saw Al Miller again. I was drenched with sweat, limping slightly from a sore hip, and flexing a freshly battered hand. My helmet and shoulder pads hung from my left hand like trophies from some distant war. It was a Wednesday afternoon, always the longest and hardest practice day of the week, and I was coming off the field amid a throng of other Falcons players. Most of us were too tired to speak. Al sat in the shade underneath the overhang just outside the locker room door, smiling brightly and nodding his head to everyone that looked his way. In his left hand was his pipe, and when he saw me, he raised it toward me as if he were making a toast.

"Looking good," he said congenially, rising to his feet. "How do you feel?"

"Worn out right now," I told him, slumping down next to where he'd been sitting on the bench.

We sat quietly together watching the last of my teammates file into the building.

"I've got what you asked for," Al said when we were alone. He extracted an envelope from the inside pocket of his sport coat. "Your father's done well."

Al handed me the packet. Inside were copies of tax rolls that showed the various office buildings and housing tracts Don Reinwulf owned and how much they were worth. Also included were some newspaper articles, a summary report, and some snapshots of his home. It was fascinating.

I looked up at Al for him to tell me more.

"The photos are where he lives," he said, leaning over to point them out. "How about that?"

I nodded. "Yeah . . . "

The home was grand. It sat like a baronial chalet atop a green hill. Behind it Mount Rainier loomed like the matriarch of all the other lesser mountains. Off to one side of the house a dark brown horse grazed by itself in a field.

"You can't even see it from the road," Al bragged. "My guy got back around behind it. After your father left college, he went to Germany, where he was stationed for a few years as an officer. He was married while he was over there, and when he came back, he and his wife went to live in Seattle. He started his own computer software company back when computers were just staring to get big. He's done well, as you can see. . . .

"I guess you don't have to worry about him wanting to ask you for a loan," he added with a soft chuckle.

"He had two kids," I said, reading into the report.

"Yeah," Al said, "you've got a sister who's not too much younger than you and a brother four years after her. I didn't have the guy go into any detail on them, or your father for that matter. He just kind of got the obvious stuff. The newspaper articles are all about some of his philanthropic things. He's been pretty active in some of those things. Otherwise, well, I guess the material speaks for itself. It's a nice success story, huh?"

I nodded.

"Al, thanks again," I said, rising to go. "I've got to get inside for a film meeting, but thanks."

"You know I'm happy to help. I must admit, since this whole thing started, I wanted to find out who he was, too. It will kind of give you some closure. When do you think you'll contact him?"

"I don't know," I said. I really didn't. "It's hard to explain. I probably will. I guess I just want to think about it . . . want to think about him. I'm glad I know, though."

Al nodded. "Well, let me know."

"I will."

Contacting my father wasn't contingent on my finding out that he was a man of wealth, but the success he obviously enjoyed and the family that he had took away any fears I'd harbored that he might be the kind of person to do something drastic when he learned about me. It wasn't that I was worried about him clinging to me for money, although I'd certainly seen enough contemporaries of mine in the NFL lose millions to parents and friends and their get-rich schemes. It was more about having the confidence that if I did contact him, I could do so without threatening Joanne's privacy. With everything Don had established in his life, it seemed highly unlikely that he would start showing up in my life uninvited after I'd made first contact.

Had he been a convicted felon or a drug addict or a derelict, I can't say for sure what I would have done. I only know this: Even though I wanted to find my father, and would have wanted to meet him even if he were a vagrant and a scoundrel, I didn't feel the same compulsion to meet him as I did to find my mother. It was she, after all, who bore me for nine months. It was she who insisted that I be placed only with college-educated parents. And it was she who was helpless to defend herself from a disapproving society that had scourged her since infancy. My father simply did what he did and went on his way.

Yet while I didn't feel compelled to contact my father in the same way I had Joanne, neither did I have any feelings of bitterness toward him. As I already said, I could easily identify with the type of behavior that could result in illegitimate children, so I was no one to judge. And I certainly never begrudged the fact that after leaving my mother in her condition, Don had gone on to achieve extraordinary financial security. I never bothered fantasizing about what might have been if they'd stayed together.

As I've said already, I wouldn't have traded lives with anyone I'd ever met, and still wouldn't to this day. The truth was, I was relieved to learn my father's situation was so comfortable. It gave me the green light to contact him, and that's what I wanted to do. Because for all the similarities I shared with my mother—and they are numerous—there were some things that were still inexplicable, loose threads in my personality that were connected to no one and nothing. There was one more person out there whose eyes I could look into and still see something of myself.

Thirty-six

When the call came from my brother Kyle's girlfriend, I wasn't home, but when I walked in the door, Illyssa told me that she'd called. I had been speaking with Kyle every few weeks since helping to capitalize his small lawn-care business. Things had gone well. During the summer, people on the coast of south Georgia were desperate to have someone take care of their lawns. Kyle always liked that sort of thing, hard physical labor and being outdoors. He got along because there was no one for him to fight with or answer to. If someone complained about the job he did, which was rare because he was so fastidious, he simply wouldn't go back. There was always someone who needed him.

Winter had always been a concern to me. Kyle wasn't one to put a tremendous amount of thought into even the immediate future, so when I brought up the fact that things would inevitably slow down once the weather turned, he wasn't interested. Then one day he announced to me that his plan for the winter was to cut firewood. It seems that even in Brunswick, Georgia, the one thing people needed as much as having their lawns attended to in the summer was a good supply of wood in the winter. Again, Kyle would work for himself and by himself. He'd purchased a chain saw with the profits from his lawn care, and he found some wooded lots that people would actually pay him to clear. His truck could move the wood. All he needed was his own strong back and a cheap ad in the paper advertising the firewood. Kyle seemed to have finally found himself, and I was as happy and proud as if he'd been named CEO of a major corporation.

All things considered, I suppose I shouldn't have been too surprised when his girlfriend called with the news. Kyle knew what I'd been doing in regards to Joanne, and he knew that I'd found her. We never spoke about it much. The times it did come up, I would change the subject. The reason I was never comfortable talking about Joanne with Kyle was the very reason his girlfriend had called. Kyle was ready to find his own biological mother, and she was going to help him. How and where, she wanted to know, should she help him begin?

"What did you tell her?" I asked Illyssa, throwing myself wearily down on the couch.

"I told her it was hard," Illyssa said.

"Good. What else?"

"I didn't know what to say," she said. "I don't know if it would be a good idea for him, but I couldn't tell her that. I told her she'd have to talk to you."

"Good," I said without having any intention of talking to her.

Since I'd found my own mother, I had heard numerous stories about other people who'd done the same. Many times things didn't work out as smoothly as they had with me and Joanne. One girl, whose father I knew, found her biological mother only to be rejected again. The mother wanted nothing to do with her daughter and was actually offended that she had shown up uninvited in her life. Another girl I knew had a biological sister sired by her father. The missing sister showed up at their doorstep one day unannounced. The whole family had nothing but resentment and scorn for the newcomer, and the father was too embarrassed to do anything to dissuade their outward disdain.

I don't know for certain what the background of my brother's parents was. I'd heard rumors in the family over the years. I heard his father was in a band. I heard his mother was on drugs. I heard things I don't want to repeat, but I never heard anything that made me want to pull out all the stops to try and help Kyle find them. I understood that with his thriving young business he was at peace with himself, maybe for the first time in his life, and that he too wanted some closure. But all I saw was the potential for heavy emotional damage with very little upside.

After what had happened to me with the woman called Martha, I knew that finding the wrong set of circumstances would be worse than going through life with that empty feeling always haunting the back of your thoughts. I guess also it was arrogance on my part to presume all along that I would find two people who were as successful and strong as my parents had turned out to be. In all honesty, I didn't think that would be the case for Kyle. I was afraid for him more than anything. These days I think maybe I was wrong. I think even if it did end up hurting him that he has a right to know. Kyle doesn't have kids of his own, and I know that those same feelings of disconnection I had he must live with every day: no past, no future. I think everyone has a right to both.

But back then, I hadn't thought it out that clearly. When Kyle's girlfriend finally did track me down on the phone, I was well prepared to rain all over her parade. I told her, not untruthfully, that it was next to impossible to find one's biological parents in New York State and that only by incredible luck, the burning of endless favors, and a prodigious amount of money could Kyle have even a slim chance of locating them. It must have worked, because she never inquired about it again.

Two years later, Kyle would show up without the girlfriend, without the truck, without the chain saw, without the riding mower, and even without the winter coat I'd given him for Christmas, and we'd talk about it. We would be in the living room of my Atlanta home during the latter part of the football season, when frost had begun to lace the dry brown lawns of our small suburban neighborhood. I would be lying on a couch and he would be on the floor, not unlike the way we used to sleep as kids when he'd sneak into my bedroom late at night and lie down next to my bed so we could talk each other to sleep. We would be half-drunk that night after me having taken him out for a steak dinner while Illyssa put our two kids and herself to bed. It would be dark in the living room except for a small swatch of light spilling down the hall from out of the kitchen. We would both have open bottles of beer in our hands. Mine would be half full, his half empty.

"I wanted to find my parents," he'd tell me without warning, broaching the subject for the first and last time, "because in a way, I don't have anyone. I know that's how you felt, but now you don't feel that way. . . . "

"You're not alone, Kyle," I would tell him, looking up through the darkness with false interest at the dimly lit shape of the ceiling fan above. "You've got me."

"You know what I mean," he would tell me, lifting his head at a hard angle off the floor to take a long swig from his bottle. "You're just my brother. Hell, you're not even that really. . . . "

"I'm your brother, Kyle," I would tell him with certainty. "I'm your brother more than most brothers who have the same blood. I'll always be your brother, man. And you'll never be alone. Not if I'm around. You aren't alone."

Kyle didn't say anything then. He just turned his head quietly away from me toward the far wall. I've never seen my brother cry and I don't know if he did then. I do know this: He believed that I loved him and that I'd always be there for him no matter what, and it was true.

Thirty-seven

After learning what my father's situation was, the more I thought about it, the more certain I was that he wasn't going to be even a remote threat to Joanne. The idea of contacting him banged around freely in my head all during the rest of that football season. Then one day when the season was over and we were back in our place up north, out of nowhere, I decided to write him a letter. I sat down at my desk in the little alcove off our bedroom and wrote.

In it, I told him who I was and what I had done with my life. I explained that in no way did I want or expect anything from him. I had plenty of money and a wonderful family around me. I also made it clear that I wasn't looking for explanations or apologies. The one thing I did ask for, though, was to meet him face-to-face and shake his hand. I wanted at least that. At the same time, I wrote that I understood completely if that was not possible.

I showed Illyssa the letter, three curling yellow handwritten pages torn from the legal pad I kept in my book bag for school.

"What do you think?"

She nodded her head slowly as she read and then handed it back to me. "It's good," she said.

"What do you think though?"

"What do you mean?"

"Do you think he'll call?" I said, stuffing the letter into an envelope and putting in one of my football trading cards for good measure, figuring it verified I was who I purported to be as well as anything.

"Yes," she told me. "He'll call you."

"You can't just go saying that," I told her. "You can't say it if it's not going to happen. Are you sure?"

"Yes, I told you. I think he'll call. He will."

He did call, and it was extraordinarily unsettling.

I was on all fours on the living room rug when the phone rang. Cody had just escaped to the other side of the couch that floated in the middle of the room in front of the TV. He was only a year old and still crawling. This was his favorite pastime.

"Tim," Illyssa said, coming out of the kitchen with her hand clamped over the phone, "I think it's him. I think it's your father. . . . "

The nerves in my stomach lit up like a stadium at a night game. "Hello?" I said, keeping my eyes on Illyssa as I spoke.

"Hi . . . Tim?" he said pleasantly.

"Yes," I said.

"This is Don Reinwulf."

"Hi."

"I got your letter."

"Yeah, I figured you did."

"You seem like a really nice young man. You've really accomplished a lot."

"Thank you," I said.

"I'm afraid you've made a mistake though," he told me gently. "There's no way I could be your father."

I started to speak, but gagged on my words instead. This I had not expected.

"You seem like a nice young man," he continued, "and I'm sure what you're trying to do is a good thing, but this is a mistake. I'm sorry."

"I . . . I don't think it's a mistake," I sputtered, giving Illyssa a puzzled look. She furrowed her brow and shook her head no. To her it wasn't a mistake, and if she felt that way, then I felt that way. Still, no matter what I said, I couldn't convince Don Reinwulf that he was my father. I carefully recalled the details of Joanne's history for him.

"Well, Tim," he said when I'd finished. "I've thought about this pretty thoroughly. I know when you were born and I went back to where I was at the time. I wasn't at the university then. I was in the military. I graduated the year before. I graduated in 1962. There's no way I could be your father."

"I'm pretty sure I'm right," I told him. "I think I am. Would you do a genetic test?"

This silenced him for a moment. Then he said, "There really isn't any sense in it. I can't be your father."

"If you're not, there really wouldn't be any harm in a test," I said, adding, "I'll pay for the whole thing. I really would like to know for sure."

"I . . . I'll have to think about all this," he said. "I have to talk to my wife about this. It's not just me that's affected by all this. I haven't thought about anything like this. I think it's a mistake. I'm sorry."

"I understand," I replied. "So, will you let me know?"

"I will," he told me. "I'll let you know."

A few days later, Don called back. I wasn't home, so he spoke sympathetically to Illyssa.

"Your husband seems like a really nice guy," he told her. "But I think he should get some psychological counseling. Obviously, he's very upset about this whole thing."

When I got home from the university, Illyssa told me, "He was very nice. He reminded me of you in that way. I mean, here you are, a total stranger to him. He really doesn't think you're his son, but he's worried about you. It just seems like something you'd do."

"I'm beginning to wonder if I'm not crazy," I told her.

"What do you mean?"

"I mean, maybe I'm wrong about this whole thing."

"How could you be wrong?" she said.

"What if he's not my father," I said. "What if Joanne just . . . just doesn't remember what really happened . . . I don't know! I don't know how or why, but what if Joanne's wrong, not Don?"

Illyssa shook her head doubtfully. "She didn't just make all this up."

"I know," I said, frustrated. "No, I don't know. Maybe she did make it up. How do we know what happened? Maybe she's wrong. Maybe it's not him. He's obviously convinced if he's recommending I get therapy, and you say he was saying it in a nice way."

"He is being nice," Illyssa said, "but that doesn't mean he's not wrong."

"Is he?" I said, looking at her incredulously. The whole thing seemed to be falling apart in my mind. If this man said he wasn't even in the country at the time, maybe Joanne had confused reality. I couldn't help remembering the woman Martha who had answered my personal ad, the one who claimed she was my mother and hadn't remembered until recently, when she was undergoing therapy, that she'd even had a son. Obviously what we were dealing with here, the bearing of and subsequent loss of a child, created emotions as volatile as a leaking nuclear reactor. Maybe it was Joanne who'd had a meltdown? I didn't think so, but I couldn't keep the idea from rearing its head.

"Yes," Illyssa told me, "he is wrong. He's nice, but he's wrong. Of course this man is your father. I'm sure more than before. The way he's dealing with this is the way you'd deal with something like this. It's not easy for him. He's got his own life and he really probably doesn't even remember what happened. It was a long time ago. But a lot of people would have hung up the phone on you and told you not to bother them. He thinks you're a little crazy, but at least he cares enough to offer his advice."

"Did he say he'd take the test?" I wanted to know.

"I told him that was all he had to do, and you'd be satisfied," Illyssa said. "I think he's going to do it, but call him and talk to him."

"I can't believe he thinks I'm crazy," I muttered as I picked up the phone and dialed.

Don was extremely nice in the way he told me a test would be for naught, but I was adamant that I wanted to go through with a genetic ID.

"Okay, so how do we do it?" he finally said.

"I'm not exactly sure," I admitted, since I hadn't looked into the details. I knew however that such a thing certainly existed. "I'll find out."

"Okay," he told me, "that sounds fine. You find out. I'll take the test."

We wrapped up our conversation in an awkward fashion, both of us glad to slip back into the comfort of our own worlds. When we talked about anything but the immediate issue of paternity, I couldn't keep myself from digging for information about his family and his own personal history, since I presumed it was part of my own. But Don didn't seem anxious to spend much time talking about my life or his, which was completely understandable. He wanted to put this whole thing behind him. He believed that once the matter of genetics was cleared up I would be just another stranger living a life that had nothing to do with his own.

I was still confused as to whether or not Joanne, because of the extreme emotional hardships she had endured, had mistaken the facts of her earlier life. It seemed possible to me, even though I doubted it, not only because of the impression I had of Joanne as an extremely competent and stable woman, but because of Illyssa's take on the whole thing. Even so, I was apprehensive about the testing, because I didn't know what I would think if it turned out Joanne was wrong and Don wasn't my father. If he wasn't, then who was? While I labored over the possibilities, there was one I never considered, so when Don called me a week later, I was stunned by the news he gave me.

Thirty-eight

"I'm sorry," Don explained, "I can't take the test. I'm sure I'm not your father anyway."

I was standing in my living room, and the baby was throwing large colorful plastic blocks at my knees. Every third or fourth toy would strike bone and bounce back at him, eliciting a squeal of delight. I had trouble getting my mind out of the gear it operated in while playing with a one-year-old. What Don was telling me didn't make any sense. How on earth could he not go through with it? If what he said was true, then he had nothing to fear. If he was right, I would gladly go my separate way. If he was wrong and Joanne was right, how could he not want to know that he had a son?

The problem was with his wife. From the beginning, Don's wife, Segrid, suspected some kind of scam. Despite the fact that I made it clear in my letter that I was financially independent and had no intention of making any claims on Don in that way, Segrid was convinced something was not right. She had urged him from the beginning to consult with a lawyer and dispose of me as quickly, efficiently, and unceremoniously as possible.

"You have to understand," Don explained again, "I can't jeopardize the family I have because of some wild thing that might be. Even if I was your father, and I'm not, what difference would it make?"

"I guess I just want to know," I responded weakly, my heart sinking like a cinder block.

"But it wouldn't change your life," he reasoned. "You've had a good life. You have a great wife and a family. Everything is good with you. You've found Joanne. Let that be enough. Go on with your life. . . . "

I felt absolutely powerless. There was nothing I could do to force Don into a blood test. All my thoughts about completing the story were ruined. I would have to live with the uncertainty and hope that over time it would become a muted cry within my mind, drowned out by the imminent events of my own young family.

"All right?" he said.

"What can I say?" I responded, trying not to be bitter. "There's nothing I can do. I think you're my father. I understand your situation and I don't expect you to ruin your own life to satisfy my curiosity, but I'd think you'd want to know, too."

"It's just not worth ruining my marriage and breaking up the family that I have. You understand that, don't you?"

"Yes," I said sullenly, "I do."

"Well . . . good luck with everything."

"Thanks," I said, and hung up.

I immediately plunked myself down on my knees and began fielding plastic blocks all over the carpet. To Cody, the phone call was only a minor disturbance in a great game. Illyssa wandered in from the kitchen. She'd watched and listened to enough of my end of the conversation from across the breakfast bar to know what had transpired. I looked up at her from the floor and she put her hands in my hair and bumped her stomach up against my head. She was about five months pregnant at the time, and her abdomen was firm against my cheek. Frustration churned beneath the surface of my face.

"He'll call you back," she said gently.

I snorted skeptically. "That's it," I told her. "That's the end. He told me. He's not calling back."

"He'll call," she said patiently. "He's not going to be able to go that long wondering whether or not you're really his son. That's your father, Tim, and he's going to call you back."

I shook my head and went on playing with our boy. Illyssa gave my hair one last tousle, then turned back toward the kitchen to finish with dinner.

■ ■ ■

A few weeks later, Joanne came for a visit. She was the consummate guest, helping Illyssa with every household task, fussing endlessly over the baby, never asking for anything. I learned since then that it was more than her trying to make a good impression. That's just her. Joanne behaves that way effortlessly, always shouldering more than her share of any burden, always cheerful and ready to laugh.

But despite the equanimity that accompanied her visit, I was ill at ease. One night, with Cody and Illyssa off to bed, Joanne and I took a walk in our modest but quiet neighborhood. Normally, I could hold her hand as comfortably as I did my own, but that night I used the brisk spring night as an excuse to keep my fists stuffed into the pockets of my jacket. As connected as I felt to Joanne, my vision of her was clouded in one corner by a web of suspicion.

I wanted to believe that everything she had told me was true. She seemed so credible. But the man she claimed to be my father seemed certain he was not, and he seemed to be as formidable an individual as she was. I couldn't broach the subject with her to test the veracity of her story either. I took my pact with her on the first night we'd spoken to mean that there was a blackout between us—not only regarding her family, but also when it came to Don.

We marched through a maze of houses that seemed cast from the same die. Several times, Joanne asked me if something was wrong. My responses were false. My part of our conversation was pure fluff. My real thoughts were floundering in a sea of doubt.

Summer soon came and I resolved the ending to my novel. Once I did that, the writing seemed to leap from my fingertips like static electricity on a winter day. It wasn't long before my first book was complete and I was ready for the next and most painful step: sending my manuscript out to publishers. I had an agent. That was the good news. Most writers struggled just to get that far.

But although an agent guaranteed that at least someone at the big publishing houses would look at my novel, it didn't mean they would actually sit down and read it from front to back. Manuscripts build up on the desks of most editors like snowfall in Syracuse on a December day. A foot-high pile isn't unusual. It doesn't take much to realize that there's no way an editor can get through every manuscript she agrees to look at. What happens usually is that they read a synopsis as well as a very small amount of the book to get a feel for the writing.

The other thing I had going for me, besides the agent, was the fact that if I could get my book published, I would be the only active NFL player to have a novel printed during his playing career. Peter Gent, who wrote *North Dallas Forty*, was the most famous football-player-turned-novelist. But Pete hadn't written his book until he'd retired from the game. I figured the novelty of my playing status, coupled with my work for National Public Radio, where I wrote commentaries about life in the NFL, would be enough for some publisher to take a chance on my book. If nothing else, they were sure to get some publicity out of it.

However, in the way that almost every football player must endure the brutality of a hot punishing training camp, almost every writer must likewise endure the brutality of rejection. One by one, copies of rejection letters to my agent would trickle in through the mail. The sense of failure was more poignant than anything I'd ever experienced in athletics. In sports, losing hurts emotionally, and being beaten physically is no great joy either, but a book is part of your soul turned inside out. To parade that out for someone sitting at a desk in some Manhattan high rise so they can sneer and dismiss you out of hand is searing.

Fortunately, I had spoken with a woman on the inside of the publishing industry who gave me some wonderful words of wisdom to bolster me. I met this woman's brother during a network television interview before a big football game. It somehow came out during the interview that I was writing a novel. The brother, who was one of the production crew, told me to call his sister if I would like some help. I did, and although she wasn't able to help me get my book published at the house where she was an editor, her words enabled me to endure the scathing rejections that took place for more than a year after I'd completed my novel.

She said, "Remember, one hundred people can say no, but if just one says yes, then you'll be a published author. Most people do hear it a hundred times, too. The difference is the people who keep going until they find that one yes."

That summer, I had no idea how many "no's" I'd have to endure, neither did I know that one day I would be a best-selling author with six-figure book deals stretching out for years into the future. What I did know was this: I was a writer. I knew it because as soon as I'd completed my first novel, I immediately set to work on another. It wasn't even a question for me. Writing had become an involuntary function in my life. I could no more imagine not working on my computer late into the night than I could not taking Illyssa out on a weekly dinner date, or reading books, or playing with my kids on the lawn, or drinking cold beer with a good friend on a summer night. Writing became synonymous with good living.

That summer came to an early close as did every summer while I was an NFL player. Training camp loomed. Illyssa and I packed up our things and prepared to depart for Atlanta for another season. It was the night before we were to head south, and I was just finishing up the first chapter of my second novel, working away on my computer in the air-conditioned alcove next to our bed, when from out of nowhere Don called.

Thirty-nine

It was just as Illyssa had said. Don couldn't escape the idea that I might be his son.

"I've thought about this a lot," he told me. "I couldn't get it off my mind, and I remembered that there was a week during that spring before you were born when I went back to the university to visit some friends, before I went to Germany. I think there was a girl who said something to me about being pregnant, I don't know for sure, but it's possible.

"Anyway, I was drinking quite a bit in those days, so I can't say for sure what might have happened."

I didn't care if he'd come to the resolution through divine intervention or by way of temporary insanity. I was only thrilled at the prospect of finding out the truth, once and for all.

"So you'll have the test?" I said.

"Yes, I'll do it."

"What about your wife?" I couldn't help asking.

"She's not happy about it," he told me, "but it'll be all right. I've talked to her about it. I've assured her that either way it won't change anything and that you don't want anything. She's just being protective of our family."

"That's understandable," I said, meaning it. "So when do you want to do this test?"

"Whenever you do."

"Okay," I said. "I'm leaving tomorrow for Atlanta for the football season. Give me a week or so to get settled in and I'll find out how this thing is done. . . . "

I didn't know what more to say, and neither did Don. Everything hinged on whether or not he was my father or the victim of a twisted recollection. If he was my father, then there was a lot for both of us to say. If he wasn't, then there was nothing. We both seemed to teeter between the two.

"All right," he said finally, "I'll wait to hear from you."

"Okay," I told him. "Thanks."

"Okay. Good-bye."

Before I left, I called the national laboratory that did all the work for the NFL drug tests and asked for some information on a genetic ID. They didn't do it, but they gave me the number of a lab that specialized in just that. I called them and arranged for blood sample kits to be sent to me at my address with the Falcons and to Don at his home. All we had to do was have a doctor take the blood and send it in. They would provide the analysis in about three weeks' time.

The next day I was on the examination table being prodded by our team doctor. He was busy processing us like turkeys before the Thanksgiving rush. There were eighty or so men who were getting ready to try to make the team, and each one had to be inspected.

"Charlie," I said to him after he'd approved the well-being of all my vital organs, "I was wondering if you could help me with something. . . . "

Charlie was a patient man, but he had bodies stacking up outside in the hall, so I teased him a little with some high points of my story.

"When I was an infant, I was adopted. Well, I think I've found the man who is my biological father, only he doesn't think he is. He lives in Seattle, and I'm going to have one of those genetic tests done to determine whether or not I'm his son. Could you take a blood sample for me and send it in to the lab?"

Hooked by the intrigue, Charlie put down his clipboard and said he'd be happy to help. He wanted to know more, despite the line outside. I filled him in briefly, and he told me to come back after lunch with the test kit.

Five weeks later, I was out of training camp and living in the house we had rented for the season. The results of the test arrived in the mail confirming that Don was my father. I called him right away.

"I know," he told me, obviously stunned, "I just got the mail. . . . "

"Well . . ." I said, unable to think of anything to say besides "I told you so" and not wanting to say that.

"I really can't believe this," Don said. "I really didn't remember."

"I know. I could tell."

He took a deep breath and exhaled into the phone. "I'd like to come and see you," he said.

"That would be great," I told him. "Why don't you come some weekend for a game?"

I told him the schedule for the next several weeks and he said he'd get back to me on exactly when he could come. Before he arrived, Illyssa gave birth to our daughter Sarah. Between the new baby and football, our lives were more than hectic. So before I knew it, I was shuffling slowly out of Atlanta Fulton County Stadium after a game against the Rams to meet the man who was my father.

Don sat packed into the front seat of a gray mid-sized rental car. He must have been exhausted from his trip, because despite being folded into the front seat like a lawn chair, his chin was resting against his chest and he was fast asleep. I rapped on the window, startling him awake. Another person might have been embarrassed, but as I was soon to learn, Don wasn't the sort to be embarrassed over anything.

He unfolded his 6'6" frame from the car, and I looked up into his eyes. Their coloring and the intensity that seemed to smolder just beneath the surface reminded me of my own. Otherwise, he was probably the last person on earth someone would presume was my father. Our physical appearances were as opposite as the similitude I shared with Joanne. Looking at him, face-to-face, eye-to-eye, I extended my hand and met his firm grip.

"It's nice to see you," I said. "I'm glad you could come."

"To be honest, I don't know what to say," he told me. "But I'm glad I'm here."

"This is Illyssa," I said, drawing her from behind me where she'd taken up hiding.

"It's very nice to meet you, Illyssa," Don said. "Where are the kids? I'd like to see them."

The kids were home with Claudine, a woman who'd been with Illyssa's family when she was growing up who had come to help us in Atlanta. Don followed us in his rental car, hunched over the wheel of a vehicle that was two sizes too small. The normal ache from being battered around the field all afternoon was nicely subdued by the foggy sensation I was feeling at having finally met both of the people responsible for my being.

"Congratulations," Illyssa said, laying her hand on my knee and giving it a gentle squeeze. "You did it. It wasn't easy, but you did it."

"Thanks," I said, glancing over at her with a small smile. "It's strange, you know. I've waited so long. I've wondered so long. . . . "

"Are you happy?" she asked.

I looked at her again, smiling big. "I'm happy I'm with you. I'm happy we've got two beautiful healthy kids. Am I happy about finding them? Yeah, of course. It's hard to explain, but it makes me feel . . . "

"Settled?"

"Yeah . . . settled," I said, knowing what she meant, no more nights lying awake thinking about where I'd come from. "Now I only have to worry about where I'm going."

"You'll go wherever you want to go," she told me. "Everything you set out to do, you always end up doing."

"That's why I married you," I said.

"Why's that?"

"Because you believe in me."

Forty

My relationship with Don took on the shape of a singular friendship. He welcomed me into his life, as did his wife and their own two children, my other half brother and half sister. Yet at the same time, there was a distance between us that didn't exist with Joanne. Nevertheless, I still see Don from time to time and speak with him occasionally on the telephone. And when we are together or speaking, it's not unusual for one of us to toss a direct line across the gulf of time, space, and circumstances that has separated us. When these moments occur, we share an eerie bond, and I think, yes, this man is my father.

I learned that his childhood, like Joanne's, was a difficult one. Alcoholism and physical abuse were the constants. At fourteen, Don left home and escaped to a Catholic school. His intelligence and his skills on the basketball court got him all the way through college despite heavy drinking and constant carousing. While he served in the army as a lieutenant, he never advanced and never cared to. He thought the whole thing was ludicrous. It was when he was stationed in Germany, however, that he met his wife. She had escaped from East Germany as a teenager. He promised her that when they went to the States, she could chose anyplace she wanted to live. Seattle seemed the perfect place to her, and Don set out to make his fortune.

While his innovation and intellect could have enabled him to grow his company into a huge corporation, he elected instead to keep things simple, using a small staff, making large deals with low over-head and socking away a fortune. Now he's given it all up for retire-ment. He viewed life somewhat like a board game and knew he could figure a way to make enough money to set himself free while at the same time refusing to play by some of the established rules. Never, even when building his business from scratch, would he join a club that was restricted. In fact, Don would go out of his way to join organizations that were normally Jewish or black. It wasn't the money or power Don was ever after, but the freedom money could bring. Thus he would never sacrifice his freedom of mind and spirit in the pursuit of money. He never had aspirations of lording over a large organization, wearing a suit. He dresses most times in sweat suits and cares nothing for status symbols. Still, he made it big.

His own drinking is no longer a problem, although he says it once was. He won't have more than a rare glass of wine anymore. He infu-riates people who know him and mystifies those who don't by speak-ing exactly what is on his mind. It's a testament to his mental powers that he ran a business at all. If he thinks someone is an ass, he tells them, in those very words. In this way, he and I couldn't be farther apart. I am a political being, and getting along or advancing my cause is far more important to me than letting someone know I think he's an ass.

There are many things, though, that I have come to see of myself in Don. I see a candor among those he loves and a willingness to ex-amine his own flaws. I see a love and appreciation for nature, books, and art. I see a fierce intellectual pride. I see a drive to compete and succeed. I see a preoccupation with self that needs at times to be checked by a strong and rational woman.

As for Joanne, the confirmation of her history made me feel slightly ashamed for ever having doubted her at all. It also made me glad. I speak to Joanne regularly and see her quite often. The connec-tion that exists between us to this day flows as naturally as a current running through braided bands of copper wire. I will probably never be able to get over my fascination at seeing slight mannerisms in her that I recognize as being identical to my own. And I know that I'll likewise never be able to look at my mother's face without the feeling that I'm looking at a reflection of myself in the uneven surface of some deep pool.

Kenny, who actually lived with Illyssa and the kids and me one summer between college semesters while working at a nearby environmental engineering firm, has become more than a brother to me. He is a friend. In fact, whenever I need to take a long road trip, as I did every year, either bringing a vehicle to or from Atlanta during or after the football season, Kenny would be the one I'd call.

Together, we'd traverse the highways up and down the Northeast, eating in truck stops and staying in cheap roadside motels, all the while kidding each other and talking about life as effortlessly as two brothers who'd grown up together in the same household. But there was only one household I grew up in, and it wasn't the same as Kenny's.

The season I met Don was also the best season I had with the Falcons. I was playing the game at my highest level and our team had finally broken the bonds of mediocrity and advanced to the NFL playoffs. We actually won the first wild card game, but then lost the next week to the eventual world-champion Washington Redskins. All the same, it was a sweet taste of excitement and nominal fame.

After the season, we returned again to upstate New York. I was weary and sore from football and glad to be returning to the less physical but more mentally challenging environs of law school. We still had our town house, but now we also had a large home we had designed and built on Canandaigua Lake, about fifty minutes from Syracuse. It was almost complete. There were only a few months we'd have to stay in the town house, and it was a good thing. We only had two small bedrooms, and with a second child, our quarters were tight. We put Cody's crib in the second bedroom and Sarah's bassinet in the alcove right off our bedroom where I did my writing.

The phone conversations I'd had with my parents during football season had been more equable than any in the past two years. Nevertheless, when I got home, since I missed Christmas because of the playoffs, it wasn't until midway through March that we even got around to arranging a dinner together. Unfortunately, our relationship, if it was healing at all, seemed to be doing so slowly. Still, I would see them. Illyssa and I planned to go out with them to dinner on a Thursday night.

On that Wednesday, both Cody and Sarah came down with the flu. They were sick all day long, alternating between fitful naps, vomiting, and crying. I was spared the worst of it because of my class and workout schedule. When I returned home for dinner, however, I knew that Illyssa was going to need a break. She sat with me at the table, almost too tired to eat.

"We'll get them to sleep," I told her, "and then you can go to bed, too."

"I will," she said, smiling weakly and pushing back a strand of dark silky hair that had fallen across her cheek.

I helped her clean up and then bathe the kids. I was the expert at putting them to sleep, so I took them one at a time and rocked them in the darkness of our bedroom in the big rocking chair that sat in the corner. Once they were both down and seemingly comfortable, I lay down beside Illyssa on our bed to give her some company while she fell asleep.

"We're supposed to have dinner with your parents tomorrow," she said wearily, as she drifted off. "You may want to call and change the night. I don't want to leave the kids if they're not better."

"Maybe they'll be better by tomorrow," I said quietly. I ran the tips of my first three fingers over the skin on her cheek, drawing up the corners of her mouth in a contented smile. Seconds later, her breathing became heavy. I lay there a while, simply enjoying, as I do to this day, the fact that I am married to this woman whom I love so deeply.

After a time, I sneaked silently into my alcove, past the bassinet, and sat down at my desk. The keyboard came to life in the darkness, and I began to write. Happily, my first novel had already been sold and I was well into my second. That night, I felt like finishing the scene I was in the middle of rather than pore through my law books. I was still working at around one in the morning when all hell broke loose.

Sarah woke up first, wanting to be fed. I did that downstairs on the couch. She promptly threw everything up and began to roar pitifully.

Her cries were enough to wake Cody. He wanted to be fed too, and he let me know it. He was also still sick. I sprinted up the stairs with Sarah in one arm and scooped Cody up in the other. I wanted to get them both downstairs to muffle the noise as much as possible so Illyssa could sleep. There was no reason for both of us to be up. I now had vomit running down my neck and inside the front of my sweat-shirt as well as a screaming child in each arm.

I propped the two of them on pillows at opposite ends of the couch, then found a quart of Pedialite on the kitchen counter and filled two bottles. Sarah took hers, but Cody shrieked. He wanted milk, but didn't know that if I gave it to him, it was going to end up on me instead of in his stomach. I immediately lifted him off the couch and began walking with him in circles, patting him gently and coaxing him to start in on the bottle of thinly flavored water.

Two hours later, after an act that I believe could only be outdone by a juggling magician, I finally had them both back to sleep. It was one of those nights that only a parent of young children can under-stand or tolerate. In the small world of my kids, everything was wrong and I was the only one on earth who could fix it. I had been tired and weary, but they needed me and I was there. I was proud of my effort. There wasn't then and there isn't now anything I wouldn't do for my children.

The next evening, I was slightly irascible. I hadn't been able to get a hold of my parents during the day to postpone our dinner, and I knew that to not show up or back out at the last moment would be tantamount to an insult. I was exhausted from the night before, and as I said, I wasn't on the most comfortable terms with my parents anyway. But I found myself in the position in which we all find our-selves at one time or another, subordinating my own wishes to peo-ple I was angry with just so they wouldn't think I was angry with them.

We met at a small Italian place that had modest prices and terrific food. Our greetings were tense, but warm nonetheless. We sat and ordered. My mother made light conversation with our waitress as she deposited a fresh, hot loaf of bread in the middle of our table. My mother's banter sounded forced. She was nervous and upset. She never did well in uncomfortable situations, and looking back, knowing the way she felt, it surprises me that she would have sat down with me at all. After all, I had opened a wound in her that remained unbreached.

After we gave our orders and the menus were laid to rest in the hands of our waitress, I cleared my throat.

"Guys," I said, addressing both my parents and clasping Illyssa's hand on the tabletop, "I want to tell you something. . . . "

I recounted for them my story from the night before, recalling the vomiting, the screaming, and my frustration in great detail.

"That," I concluded, "is what it means to be a parent. I know that now. I know what being a parent is about. It's being there when no one else wants to and when no one else can."

My mother nodded somberly and bit down on her lower lip. My father looked hard at his bread plate. Their hands met atop the table the same way mine and Illyssa's had.

"Yes it is," my mother said almost defiantly.

"I want you to know that I know that," I said. Tears built up in my eyes, as they were in everyone's.

"You guys are my parents," I said. "You're the only parents I ever had, and you're the only parents I ever will have. . . . "

My father closed his eyes briefly and my mother shook with emotion.

"I'm so glad you said that," she said to me. "I'm so glad. . . . "

Illyssa squeezed my hand and dabbed at her own tears with a napkin. I wiped my eyes on my sleeve and heaved a sigh of relief. The sensation of a heavy burden being lifted from my chest was as unmistakable as the smell of the hot bread. Whatever damage had been done could now begin to mend.

Epilogue

I had no intention of writing this book. I was trying to get Judith Regan to buy my future novels when the discussion somehow turned to her son.

"You remind me of him," she said. "He's an athlete too, and good in school. I see things in him that I can relate directly back to me, and other things that are completely his father. I'll bet you had that growing up. . . . "

"No," I said, "not really, but I know exactly what you mean."

Judith looked at me quizzically, and I explained by telling her my story.

"Now that's a book I'll buy right now," she said.

She wasn't kidding.

My parents and I see each other just about every week now. My relationship with them has never been better. Of course, we still have our occasional differences, what family doesn't? At the time I am writing this, they have yet to meet Joanne and her husband. I expect, however, that by the time you read it they will have met. They have to. All of them are part of my life and part of my children's lives. (We're expecting our fourth.) Don, too, I'm sure will one day meet my parents, although I'm almost certain he and Joanne will never cross paths.

I think my appearance has not been easy in many ways for my half siblings. I sprung up from nowhere, taking a share of their parents' attentions without ever having exposed them to my own day-to-day foibles and idiosyncrasies. I've given their parents something to be proud of without having caused them a moment's grief for at least twenty-six years. Still, everyone seems to be accepting, even though, except for Kenny, we all seem to have gone on with our separate lives.

My brother Kyle and my sister Laurie are exactly where and what they've always been. Laurie lives in Liverpool not far from my parents. We see each other during all the holidays, although not too often in between. I'm there for her, though, and she for me. Kyle is Kyle. He lives in the next town over from us and is still in a constant state of flux. At this particular moment, he has a small landscaping business that seems to be thriving. Next year, it may be something altogether different, although he seems to be as good as he's ever been. I told him the other day about the state registry for nonidentifying information.

The people who have surprised me most in all this have been the spouses of my biological parents. Joanne's husband, Ed, and Don's wife, Segrid, have been wonderful in their acceptance of me, Illyssa, and the kids. I would think that of anyone in all this, they might have the most reason to begrudge what I've done, upsetting the equilibrium of their lives. But in complete honesty, they have been great.

As for me, my life is quite different because of all this. The nightmares are gone. I can't even remember the last one. I know it was sometime before I found Joanne. I still have great aspirations in television, in books, even in movies and possibly one day in politics. I'll never be able to shake the habit of collecting different merit badges and thereby different sets of life's many experiences. But more than anything these days, I am intent on being a father and a husband. The focus of my world is my family, everything else comes after. While I want the other things to happen, and while I think they probably will, I don't *need* them to happen. All I *need* is for my family to be well, so I give them more attention than anything else.

During football season, I travel on weekends to announce NFL games for FOX, but this leaves me home all week. Once football is over, except for an occasional day out on the road for ABC News, I'm home most of the time writing into the late hours of the night. This means that during the day I get to change diapers, coach Little League, shop for groceries, take the kids to school in the morning, play chess, go hunting and fishing, swim, take Illyssa out to lunch, read books to the kids, look for frogs and crayfish, build birdhouses, go on picnics, work out, ride bikes, throw balls, rent movies, go on double dates, windsurf, read, and camp out in the backyard.

I am at peace now, maybe for the first time in my life. I hope that doesn't take away the edge that enabled me to succeed in football and school and to land jobs as a writer and in television, but if it does, it does. I have my house on the lake that I earned with the sweat and blood and bones of my body. I have my loyal wife and my beautiful kids, gifts from God. I know they love me now, and I know they'll love me forever, no matter what. I don't have to do anything or be anything. For the first time in my life, all the merit badges, honors, awards, and achievements are nothing more than trinkets on my wall. They love me simply because I'm me. Before I found Illyssa and filled in the pieces of my past, I didn't know if I ever could have felt this way. I think what happened was that when I set out to find my biological mother, I was really looking for myself.

It feels good to be home.